Lazarus
Awakening

Study Guide

Lazarus Awakening

Study Guide

*Discovering the Life You
Were Always Meant to Live*

JOANNA WEAVER

WATERBROOK

LAZARUS AWAKENING STUDY GUIDE

Trade Paperback ISBN 978-0-307-73164-7
eBook ISBN 978-0-307-73167-8

Published in the United States by WaterBrook, an imprint of Random House, a division of Penguin Random House LLC.

WATERBROOK® and its deer colophon are registered trademarks of Penguin Random House LLC.

147028622

Letter from Joanna

I'm so grateful you've chosen to study my book *Lazarus Awakening: Finding Your Place in the Heart of God.*

When my publisher asked me to expand the original Bible study and add video sessions, I could hardly wait—especially when they gave me the go-ahead to film the teaching sessions in Israel. Three years ago my husband, John, and I visited the Holy Land for the first time. Everywhere we went, I saw lessons from Lazarus and analogies that point to the resurrection life God wants to bring to every one of us. Now I have a chance to share them with you!

Just as Jesus called Lazarus out of his grave, I believe He desires to call you and me out of our tombs as well. Out of the caves of self-protection and halfway living we often settle for and into the abundant life He came to give. So that you and I become wide-awake believers—made fully alive as God intends us to be!

Over the next eight weeks, I want us to invite the Holy Spirit into every corner of our hearts, allowing the spotlight of heaven to show us places that need the touch of God. But doing that will require courage at times, my friend. For we must be willing to acknowledge any weak spots the Spirit reveals, if we are to walk out of the darkness of tombs into the glorious light of resurrection life.

In some ways, this study is the most personal one I've ever written. You'll be asked questions that don't necessarily have easy answers. And throughout the study, I'll ask you to interact with God in prayer. Please don't rush through or skip over those parts. For it is only as we allow God to search our hearts, that He's able to reveal—and then heal!—the sin-sick places in us all.

Freedom awaits each one of us as we set our minds on studying God's Word and willingly open our hearts to the Holy Spirit's work. For Love is calling our names . . .

It's time to "come forth"!

Becoming His,

Joanna Weaver

He who has the Son has life; he who does not have the Son of God does not have life.

1 JOHN 5:12

How to Use This Study

Lazarus Awakening—The Book

While you'll learn a great deal from watching the video sessions and completing the study guide homework, please be sure to read your assigned chapters in *Lazarus Awakening* prior to each week's discussion. The book provides the framework of this study and is necessary to your getting the most out of our time together.

Important note: the paperback edition of *Lazarus Awakening* includes a bonus chapter, which is intended to be read following chapter 8. If you are using the hardcover edition, you can access the bonus chapter at LazarusAwakening.com.

As early in the study week as possible, you'll want to complete your assigned reading in the book with a pen or highlighter in hand. I encourage you to mark or underline things that really speak to you—verses, quotes, stories, or analogies. Make notes in the margins of any thoughts, questions, or revelations you'd like to discuss or share in class. In order to finish the book in eight weeks, at times you'll be asked to read two chapters instead of one. Be sure to plan enough time so that you get the most out of your reading.

The Study Guide

After you've read the assigned portion in the book, begin to work through the questions and exercises in this guide. They are designed to help you reflect on God's Word and apply it. (Please note that I quote primarily from the 1984 edition of the New International Version, and most questions are shaped around that translation.)

Each week's lesson also includes:

- *an "Israel Moment" sidebar.* Designed to complement my video discussions with Amy Turnage, Director of Operations at the Center for Holy Lands Studies, these sidebars offer insights into the land that shaped Jesus and His ministry. The first three weeks also feature a "Word Time" sidebar outlining ways to go deeper in your walk with God. Corresponding videos will be shown in class if there is time. (Videos can be accessed at LazarusAwakening.com.)

- *a "Make a Plan" assignment.* Each week, you'll be encouraged to come up with action steps to apply the truths you've learned as you follow through on that plan during the upcoming week.

- *a "Who I Am in Christ" journal prompt.* Part of stepping out of our tombs involves allowing God to redefine us and replace lies with truth. Each week, you'll be asked to respond prayerfully to that process.

- *a memory verse.* Over the course of the study, you'll be asked to memorize seven verses. If that seems too overwhelming, choose one or two verses to focus on. Don't worry; I'll share some memorizing techniques that have helped me!

- *a video guide.* With fill-in-the-blank prompts, these pages help capture key points from the DVD session so that you can refer to them later.

- *a "Closing Time" reflection.* At the end of each lesson you'll have a chance to respond to what the Lord has impressed on your heart throughout the week and in the teaching session.

Note to Leaders

You'll find a comprehensive Leader's Guide on the third DVD, designed to help you navigate the special features of this study as well as get the most out of your weekly time together. Just print the pages and place them in a three-ring binder for easy use. The Leader's Guide includes:

- practical advice for leading Bible studies
- a list of DVD content, including bonus features and how to use them
- session-by-session scripts to help you lead the discussion for a two-hour class (with modifications for a one-hour class); includes video prompts and other activities
- optional Retreat Guide providing the tools you'll need to create a special event, including promotional materials, suggested activities, and lots more

The Leader's Guide can also be downloaded at LazarusAwakening.com, where additional resources are available, including memory verses, a promotional video, publicity pieces, and website graphics. You can explore my other books and video curriculums there as well.

Note: If you don't have enough time to view the bonus videos during class, please let participants know they can view the "Israel Moments" and "Word Time" videos at the website.

If you have any questions, please send me an e-mail by clicking on Connect with Joanna at LazarusAwakening.com. I hope you'll send me a note to let me know when your group will be doing the study. I'd treasure the opportunity to pray for you and inform you when any new products or study resources become available. I'd also love to hear about your study and any creative ideas you're using, as well as what God is doing in your group.

Introduction

*Now a man named Lazarus was sick. He was from Bethany, the village
of Mary and her sister Martha. . . . So the sisters sent word to Jesus,
"Lord, the one you love is sick."*

JOHN 11:1, 3

D o you ever feel stuck in your Christian walk? A bit tired and defeated? As
though you have one foot in new life while the other seems mired in the
old? Do you struggle to believe that God could love you in spite of your flaws and
failings? I know I have at times. Though I've experienced a lot of freedom through
God over the years, certain places in my soul still need to hear the good news.

The story of Lazarus shouts hope to our anxious hearts: *"You are loved. You
are accepted."* No matter the impossibility of our situations or the state of our souls,
this story reminds each one of us that we can send word to Jesus as Mary and
Martha did in John 11:3: "Lord, the one you love is sick."

Like these two sisters, we can cry out to our Savior. We can ask Him to come
to the sin-marred places in our hearts and bring life to the deadness in our souls. For
Jesus is the resurrection and the life (John 11:25). He is everything we need.

There is no tomb our Savior cannot open. There's no heart He cannot heal.
And no matter the mistakes or pain of your past, I can promise you this: there is
life on the other side of the stone that entombs you. Abundant life and glorious
freedom!

So are you ready, my friend? It's time to learn what it means to truly live.

Theme Verse

The thief does not come except to steal, and to kill,
and to destroy. I have come that they may have
life, and that they may have it more abundantly.

JOHN 10:10, NKJV

Word Time: Scripture Memorization

When we memorize scripture, it becomes a tool in our arsenal to fight off discouragement, replace lies with truth, and wage war against the enemy.

Here's a method that's really helped me:[1]

- Start by saying the reference and the first phrase together three times.
- Now add another phrase to the verse, and repeat it three times.
- If needed, repeat the second phrase alone three times.
- Add the next phrase, then repeat that portion three times.
- Now put it all together, adding the reference at the end. It will sound like this.

> (John 10:10) "The thief does not come except to steal, and to kill, and to destroy. I have come that they may have life, and that they may have it more abundantly" (John 10:10).

Here are some additional tips:

1. Review the verse regularly using this pattern:
   REFERENCE—VERSE—REFERENCE.
2. Carry a copy of each verse on an index card or in your phone.
3. Meditate on the verse. Really think about what it means. Allow it to become part of your life.

For easy reference, you'll find all of the assigned memory verses on page 121. You can also download and print them on business card stock at LazarusAwakening.com.

Do not let this Book of the Law depart from your mouth; meditate on it day and night, so that you may be careful to do everything written in it. Then you will be prosperous and successful.

JOSHUA 1:8

ISRAEL MOMENT: *The Fifth Gospel*

Each week in this sidebar and the companion video, I'll interview Amy Turnage from the Center for Holy Lands Studies.[2] (Videos available at Lazarus Awakening.com.) She loves Israel, this land referred to as the "Fifth Gospel."

> Five gospels record the life of Jesus. Four you will find in books, and the one you will find in the land they call Holy. Read the fifth gospel and the world of the four will open to you.[3]
>
> —Attributed to Saint Jerome, fifth century AD

"Map of Israel in the New Testament," courtesy of Bible History Online.
For other Bible study helps, visit: www.Bible-History.com.

DISCUSSION QUESTIONS

1. Before we begin studying this family from Bethany, share what your family of origin was like. Where do you fall in the birth order? How has it affected you?

2. Read the story of Lazarus found in John 11:1–12:11 (or on page 117 in the back of this guide). What stands out to you most in this story, and why?

Personal Survey

This week, you'll read about the love-doubt that I believe plagues many of us, even as Christians. Please give an honest evaluation of where you feel you are in your relationship with God. As you consider the following statements, rate each with: O (Often); S (Sometimes); N (Never).

_____ I regularly sense/experience God's love for me.

_____ I feel distant from God.

_____ I feel secure in God's love.

_____ I think God loves me, but I don't feel it in my heart.

_____ I believe God loves other people, but I'm not entirely convinced He loves me.

_____ I'm learning to rely on God's love rather than my own worthiness.

_____ I feel God loves me less because of past failures and mistakes.

_____ I believe I am chosen and dearly loved by God.

Stuck Christianity

For great is your love toward me; you have delivered me from the depths of the grave.

PSALM 86:13

The Story, Luke 10:38–42 and John 11:5

We can understand why Jesus loved . . .

- Mary; look how she worshiped.
- Martha; look how she _____.

The only thing of significance Lazarus did was _____, yet "Jesus loved Martha and her sister and Lazarus" (John 11:5).

From Death to Life, John 11:1–44

In many ways, the story of Lazarus parallels our salvation experience:

1. Jesus calls our _____.

2. We must respond.

3. We must _____ into new life.

4. We must begin to _____ our graveclothes.

The Invitation, John 11:25–28

"I am the resurrection and the life." (John 11:25)

"Do you _____ this?" (verse 26)

"Place of Lazarus" or *Eleazar*, which means "God has _____."

Notes

(For additional note-taking pages, see page 135.)

Closing Time

I sense the Lord saying . . .

Make a Plan

As we begin this study, write down areas in your life that need the resurrection touch of Jesus. Throughout this study, bring these areas to the Lord, inviting Him to have His way in your life.

Is there any area of fear or resistance to God's work that might hold you back?

What one thing could you do this week to break through that resistance and/or fear?

Take what you've discovered in this exercise to the Lord in prayer.

Prayer Requests

This Week's Assignment

- Follow through with your week 1 "Make a Plan" homework.
- Read chapters 1 and 2 in *Lazarus Awakening*.
- Answer week 2 study questions.
- Memorize **John 10:10** (NKJV): "The thief does not come except to steal, and to kill, and to destroy. I have come that they may have life, and that they may have it more abundantly."

Tale of the Third Follower

Jesus loved Martha and her sister and Lazarus.

JOHN 11:5

READ: Chapters 1 and 2 in *Lazarus Awakening*

Lazarus. It's amazing the things we can learn from a man who never says a word in Scripture, never does any mighty acts of faith.

When it comes right down to it, the only thing of any significance that Lazarus did was die. And yet, John 11:5 tells us, "Jesus loved Martha and her sister and Lazarus." Which means there is hope for you and me! No matter the condition or situation we may find ourselves in at the moment, no matter how small the amount of faith we bring to the relationship, you and I are loved by Jesus.

You are not a constant disappointment to God, nor a nagging obligation He can't escape, as my friend Kim Trihey described the distance she used to feel.[4] Instead, you are His beloved child. And that, dear brother or sister, is very good news!

For the same Love that came to Lazarus's rescue that long ago day in Bethany wants to rescue us as well. Whether we're entombed by past failures, bound up by fear or debilitating doubt, Jesus has come to set us free! And the one whom the Son sets free, Jesus reminds us in John 8:36, "will be free indeed."

No more doubt. No more distance. Instead, we're invited to rest as well as live in the loving embrace of God.

Memory Verse

The thief does not come except to steal, and to kill, and to destroy. I have come that they may have life, and that they may have it more abundantly.

JOHN 10:10, NKJV

Word Time: Journaling Resurrection

David's psalms are, in a sense, his journal where he poured out his heart to God. I've found that putting a pen to paper has brought a deeper dimension to my Christian walk as well. I hope you'll consider incorporating journaling into your quiet time.

Here are a few tips on dialoguing with God that have helped me:

1. *Be honest.* David didn't edit himself; he simply poured out his heart. A journal is a place where we can be real with God so that He becomes more real to us.

2. *Allow God to speak to you.* When you sense the Holy Spirit speaking truth to your situation, write down those thoughts in your journal.

3. *Remember what God has done.* Journaling helps us remember God's faithfulness in the past. Record answers to prayers so that you can return to them when new challenges arise.

There is so much power in having a living, breathing conversation with the Lord. A lot of our confusion and emotional turmoil is internal. Spilling it out on paper before the Lord never fails to bring a release for me. I pray you'll find this type of journaling beneficial as well.

"Who I Am in Christ" Journal Prompts

The enemy of our souls would like nothing more than to make us forget who we are as children of God. If he can keep us from realizing our identity in Christ, he can keep us captive to fear and self-doubt. Entombed in past failures, we'll remain bound by strongholds and unhealthy behaviors.

At the end of each week's lesson, you'll be asked to choose one of the truths listed in the "Who I Am in Christ" sidebar, found on pages 20–21 of this week's study. With the Holy Spirit's help, work through the listed questions, writing out your honest responses in the form of a prayer.

ISRAEL MOMENT: *Jesus, the Man*

We all are shaped by the places we were raised and by the people who surrounded us. Though Jesus was fully God, He was also fully man. In this "Israel Moment," Amy Turnage and I talk about the Galilean region and culture that shaped our Savior.

Region: Galilee includes a significant part of northern Israel. Nazareth, Jesus's hometown, was very small. Jesus may have spent time in Sepphoris, a large city an hour-and-a-half walk away.

Religion: First-century Galilee was a thoroughly pious Jewish region, as proved by the many ritual immersion baths, and other Jewish artifacts discovered there. It was the second largest center of religious learning after Jerusalem.

Education: In the light of first-century Judaism, the Gospels point to Jesus having had an outstanding Jewish education. Josephus mentions this in his *Testimonium Flavianum:* "At this time there was a wise man who was called Jesus. And his conduct (lit: way of life) was good and his learning outstanding."[5]

Language: Israel was trilingual in the first century. The primary language was Hebrew, but Aramaic and Greek were also spoken. Jesus alluded to the Greek fables of Aesop (the reed and John the Baptist in Matthew 11:7; the parable of the miser in Matthew 25:14–30).[6]

Father: Joseph, who appears to have died prior to Jesus's public ministry, was a carpenter (Matthew 13:55) as was Jesus (Mark 6:3). In Jewish culture, people turned to them for advice, saying, "Is there a carpenter among us, or the son of a carpenter, who can solve the problem for us?"[7]

Family: Jesus was born into a very pious Jewish family. After Jesus's birth, Joseph and Mary observed customs commanded in the Law of Moses (purification rites in Leviticus 12:1–8; first-born son payment in Numbers 18:14–16). Another sign of devotion was their yearly trip "to Jerusalem for the Feast of the Passover" (Luke 2:41), a trip most Jews made only once every few years.

This Week's Study

1. Read the story of Lazarus found in John 11:1–37. Which one of the many characters mentioned in the passage (disciples, Mary, Martha, Lazarus, Jewish bystanders) do you relate to most? Why?

2. Look at the sidebar titled "What Kind of Father Do You Have?" on pages 4 and 5 of *Lazarus Awakening*. Which (if any) misrepresentation of God as Father have you struggled with?

   How has it affected you?

   In what ways, positive or negative, has your connection with your earthly father affected your relationship with God?

3. Take a moment and read the passage below aloud, slowly and thoughtfully. Circle or underline words and phrases that stand out to you.

I pray that from his glorious, unlimited resources he will empower you with inner strength through his Spirit. Then Christ will make his home in your hearts as you trust in him. Your roots will grow down into God's love and keep you strong. And may you have the power to understand, as all God's people should, how wide, how long, how high, and how deep his love is. May you experience the love of Christ, though it is too great to understand fully. Then you will be made complete with all the fullness of life and power that comes from God. (Ephesians 3:16–19, NLT)

What in this passage speaks most to you, and why?

How would your life be different if you could get the fact God loves you from your head to your heart?

4. If you were to send a message to Jesus concerning your current situation and need, how would you finish the following sentence? (With Philippians 4:6 in mind, take what you write down to God in prayer.)

   Lord, the one you love is . . .

5. In chapter 2, I wrote about the worst sickness of all: sin-sickness. Match the downward spiral of sin and its effects listed below to the following scriptures by filling in the appropriate letter in the blank before the phrase: (a) Psalm 106:43; (b) Acts 8:23; (c) James 1:14–15.

_____ Fills us with bitterness

_____ Makes us waste away

_____ Ends in death

_____ Entices with our own evil desires

_____ Holds us captive

_____ Causes us to rebel against God

6. On the next page, read the sidebar "What God Does with Our Sins." Draw a ♡ around the three points that speak most powerfully to you. Choose one point to meditate on—really allow yourself to soak in its truth. Write out the words below. (Hey, you might even want to sketch or paint them, sing or declare them aloud!)

Look up the scripture listed with that truth, then write it in your own words:

What God Does with Our Sins

Rosalind Goforth, a well-known missionary to China, struggled many years with an oppressive burden of guilt and sin that left her feeling like a spiritual failure. Finally, out of desperation, she sat down with her Bible and a concordance, determined to find out how God views the faults of His children. At the top of the paper, she wrote these words: "What God Does with Our Sins." Then she searched the Scriptures, compiling this list of seventeen truths:

1. He lays them on His Son—Jesus Christ (Isaiah 53:6).
2. Christ takes them away (John 1:29).
3. They are removed an immeasurable distance—as far as east is from west (Psalm 103:12).
4. When sought for [they] are not found (Jeremiah 50:20).
5. The Lord forgives them (1 John 1:9; Ephesians 1:7; Psalm 103:3).
6. He cleanses them all away by the blood of His Son (1 John 1:7).
7. He cleanses them as white as snow or wool (Isaiah 1:18; Psalm 51:7).
8. He abundantly pardons them (Isaiah 55:7).
9. He tramples them underfoot (Micah 7:19).
10. He remembers them no more (Hebrews 10:17; Ezekiel 33:16).
11. He casts them behind His back (Isaiah 38:17).
12. He casts them into the depths of the sea (Micah 7:19).
13. He will not impute [or charge] us with sins (Romans 4:8).
14. He covers them (Romans 4:7).
15. He blots them out (Isaiah 43:25).
16. He blots them out [like] a thick cloud (Isaiah 44:22).
17. He blots out even the proof against us, nailing it to His Son's cross (Colossians 2:14).[8]

Blessed is he whose transgressions are forgiven,
whose sins are covered.

PSALM 32:1

7. Over and over in the Bible, we are told to "Wake up!" (Revelation 3:2). How do distractions, deceptions, doubts, disappointments, or dullness tend to lull you to sleep spiritually?

8. Consider the following verses. According to these scriptures, why is it so important that we wake up, and what should our awakening involve?

   Matthew 25:1–13

   Ephesians 5:8–15

9. "God is not mad at you!" Someone has said that's the best part of the gospel. Instead of holding a grudge against us, the Lord wants to forgive and make us His own. Look up the following scriptures and really meditate on them. Under each reference, write down key words or phrases that reveal God's attitude toward you.

   Isaiah 44:21–22

2 Corinthians 5:17–21

Colossians 2:13–15

10. As we begin this study, let's give God permission to do whatever He needs to do in order to give us the life we need. Write a prayer of consecration below, committing yourself to cooperate with the empowering grace the Holy Spirit provides.

Make a Plan

Revelation 12:11 tells us that one way Christians overcome the enemy is "by the word of their testimony." Take a moment and write out how you accepted Jesus as your Savior. It's okay if you can't remember the details; declaring your decision is the goal.

Note: If you haven't yet received the gift Jesus offers, why not do it today? Prayerfully go through the steps listed in "The Invitation" sidebar found on page 27 of *Lazarus Awakening*.

My Testimony:

Consider sharing your testimony with a friend this week. Something powerful happens when we voice what Jesus has done for us!

Who I Am in Christ ...

Choose one of the statements from the "Who I Am in Christ" sidebar on pages 20–21 to meditate on. Write out the statement and the words of the accompanying verse. Work through the questions, then respond to God in prayer concerning the truth you've discovered.

Statement:

Verse:

What lie keeps you from accepting this as truth?

What does God's Word say about that?

Prayer:

Who I Am in Christ

Ever since Adam and Eve bit into the forbidden fruit, humanity has struggled with an identity crisis. We've forgotten who we really are—chosen and beloved children of God. Consider the following list of scriptures from the wonderful devotional *One Day at a Time.*[9]

I Am Accepted

John 1:12	I am God's child.
John 15:15	I am Christ's friend.
Romans 5:1	I have been justified.
1 Corinthians 6:17	I am united with the Lord, and I am one spirit with Him.
1 Corinthians 6:20	I have been bought with a price. I belong to God.
1 Corinthians 12:27	I am a member of Christ's body.
Ephesians 1:1	I am a saint.
Ephesians 1:5	I have been adopted as God's child.
Ephesians 2:18	I have direct access to God through the Holy Spirit.
Colossians 1:14	I have been redeemed and forgiven of all my sins.
Colossians 2:10	I am complete in Christ.

I Am Secure

Romans 8:1–2	I am free from condemnation.
Romans 8:28	I am assured that all things work together for good.
Romans 8:31–34	I am free from any condemning charges against me.
Romans 8:35–39	I cannot be separated from the love of God.
2 Corinthians 1:21–22	I have been established, anointed, and sealed by God.

Colossians 3:3	I am hidden with Christ in God.
Philippians 1:6	I am confident that the good work God has begun in me will be perfected.
Philippians 3:20	I am a citizen of heaven.
2 Timothy 1:7	I have not been given a spirit of fear but of power, love, and a sound mind.
Hebrews 4:16	I can find grace and mercy to help in the time of need.
1 John 5:18	I am born of God, and the evil one cannot touch me.

I Am Significant

Matthew 5:13–14	I am the salt and light of the earth.
John 15:1, 5	I am a branch of the true vine, a channel of His life.
John 15:16	I have been chosen and appointed to bear fruit.
Acts 1:8	I am a personal witness of Christ.
1 Corinthians 3:16	I am God's temple.
2 Corinthians 5:17–21	I am a minister of reconciliation for God.
2 Corinthians 6:1	I am God's coworker (see 1 Corinthians 3:9).
Ephesians 2:6	I am seated with Christ in the heavenly realm.
Ephesians 2:10	I am God's workmanship.
Ephesians 3:12	I may approach God with freedom and confidence.
Philippians 4:13	I can do all things through Christ, who strengthens me.

I give them eternal life, and they shall never perish;
no one can snatch them out of my hand.

John 10:28

Session Two Video

Talitha Koum!

Wake up, O sleeper, rise from the dead, and Christ will shine on you.

EPHESIANS 5:14

A Family in Need, John 11:1–11

The family in Bethany sent word to Jesus . . .

- The Problem: "Lord, the one you love is _____" (verse 3).

- The Declaration: "This sickness will not end in death" (verse 4).

- The Miracle: "I am going there to _____ him up" (verse 11).

Our Touchable Jesus

Two different people from opposite ends of society, both of whom needed Jesus's touch:

- Jairus
- Unnamed woman

Pathway to a Miracle, Mark 5:22–43

1. Reach out and _____ Jesus.

   Principle #1: You matter to God.

   Principle #2: You are never a bother to God.

2. Don't be afraid; just _____.

3. It's time to _____ _____!

Mark 5:41: He took her by the hand and said to her, "Talitha koum!" (which means, "Little girl, I say to you, get up!").

Notes

Closing Time

I sense the Lord saying . . .

Prayer Requests

This Week's Assignment

- Follow through with your week 2 "Make a Plan" homework.
- Read chapter 3 in *Lazarus Awakening*.
- Answer week 3 study questions.
- Continue to review **John 10:10** (NKJV). Memorize **John 1:12:** "Yet to all who received him, to those who believed in his name, he gave the right to become children of God."

Our Friend Lazarus

*A man who has friends must himself be friendly, But there is a friend
who sticks closer than a brother.*

PROVERBS 18:24, NKJV

READ: Chapter 3 in *Lazarus Awakening*

Friendship. We all long for someone to connect with on a deeper level than that of mere acquaintance. We all need a safe place to rest our hearts.

To think that we might provide such a place for Jesus is a sobering yet exhilarating thought. For we were made for relationship with God, and our spirits know it. We were made to walk and talk with Him as intimately as Adam and Eve fellowshipped with their Maker in the garden.

Because of Jesus, we can enjoy that kind of friendship—the kind God had in mind when He first made us. For when we were unable to get up to Him, God came down to us in the person of His Son. With his final breath on the cross, Jesus removed all the hindrances and roadblocks caused by sin and tore the veil that had separated us from God (Mark 15:37–38).

In doing so, Jesus "reconciled us" to our Father (2 Corinthians 5:18), clearing the way for each of us to enter into the deepest kind of intimacy humanity could ever know: friendship with our Maker. Intimacy with the One who knows us best yet loves us most.

Memory Verse

Yet to all who received him, to those who believed in his name, he gave the right to become children of God.

JOHN 1:12

Word Time: Bible Reading Highlights

The Bible tells us that Jesus often withdrew to solitary places to communicate with His Father. I'd like to challenge you to do the same thing.

Though I've never heard the audible voice of God, the following Bible reading method has really helped me quiet my soul so I can discern God's voice as I spend time with Him each day.

- First, I ask the Holy Spirit to guide me, to give me an open mind and an open heart to see what He wants to show me in His Word.
- Rather than reading multiple chapters, I read only one. Taking my time, I read slowly, meditating on each word and thought.
- When a verse catches my attention, I stop reading and write the verse down word for word in my journal, including the reference.
- I ask God to give me wisdom and insight into the scripture and to show me how to apply it to my life.
- My thoughts often come out as a prayer. I converse with God about what I've read, thanking Him for what He has revealed.

The words in the Bible, written so very long ago, have the power to radically change your life and mine. When we take time to study Scripture, we'll find ourselves transformed into the new creations God wants us to be (2 Corinthians 5:17).

Because that's the power of God's holy Word.

In the back of this study guide, on page 123, you'll find several "Bible Reading Highlights" templates to help you capture the truths God speaks to you during your quiet time.

I run in the path of your commands,
for you have set my heart free.

Psalm 119:32

ISRAEL MOMENT: *Lessons from the Desert*

Somewhere in the 930 square miles that lie between Jerusalem's eastern edge and the Dead Sea, Jesus was led by "the Holy Spirit" into the wilderness to be tested for forty days (Luke 4:1–2). Amy Turnage shares some of the desert lessons God wants to teach us as well.

> You shall remember all the way which the Lord your God has led you in the wilderness these forty years, that He might humble you, testing you, to know what was in your heart, whether you would keep His commandments or not. (Deuteronomy 8:2, NASB)

God trained three of His greatest leaders in the desert: Abraham, Moses, and David. Perhaps it's because the desert is the "great equalizer," as Amy Turnage says, teaching us both humility and hospitality.

- *Humility:* In the desert, you need help to survive. You need water, food, protection, guidance—you need God. In the desert, everyone has the same standard of living. Today's traditional Bedouins (Arab desert dwellers) live in tents of the same size, made with the same cloth and decorations. Everyone wears the same style and type of clothing. No one lives more ostentatiously than another or flaunts his or her family wealth.
- *Hospitality:* In the desert, we are expected to be hospitable, even to our enemies. Within the Bedouin culture, a stranger is permitted lodging for three days without question—without giving his name or offering payment. Those living in the desert understand the importance of hospitality because they know they will need it one day. Showing hospitality is considered an opportunity to honor God.

Lessons from the wilderness. The desert is God's classroom. Jesus experienced it. So did Paul and other great heroes of our faith. Perhaps you've never considered that the dry, arid times in your life might just be part of God's plan for you. If we're willing to cooperate, God wants to teach us lessons there that will help us bloom where we are planted—no matter how dry and lifeless that place seems to be.

THIS WEEK'S STUDY

1. Describe a moment—big or small—when you felt especially loved. What were the circumstances, and what people were involved? Why do you think that experience was so special to you?

2. Take the test found in the sidebar titled "What Kind of Friend Am I?" on the next page. What did you discover about your relationship with God?

   What did you discover about your relationship with others?

   Share one aspect of friendship in which you'd like to grow, and why.

What Kind of Friend Am I?

We've all had needy, clinging friends who tend to take more than they give to the relationship. Though it might be a little painful, consider the following qualities of a good friend as they relate to your relationship with God. How do you rate? Mark each characteristic with a 5 (Always), 4 (Usually), 3 (Sometimes), 2 (Rarely), or 1 (Never).

_____ **Good listener:** Interested in how the other person is doing. Asks good questions. Hears the other person out; doesn't interrupt. Cares about that person's feelings. Comfortable with silence.

_____ **Low maintenance:** Isn't overly needy. Secure in self and friendship, not demanding. Doesn't need constant attention. Isn't threatened by time apart.

_____ **Not easily offended:** Patient when needs aren't immediately met. Believes the best, not the worst, of the other person. Doesn't jump to conclusions. Willing to talk things out.

_____ **Available:** Always there when needed. Willing to set aside own plans in order to help a friend. Returns calls quickly and doesn't ignore e-mails.

_____ **Not jealous:** Doesn't get mad when time is spent with other people or someone else gets a nicer birthday gift. Doesn't give the cold shoulder or leave nasty notes when upset.

_____ **Kind:** Quick with genuine words of affection and affirmation. Looks for practical ways to express love. Gentle sweetness creates a haven of safety.

_____ **Trustworthy:** Can be trusted with delicate information and difficult situations. Doesn't participate in gossip. Will not betray a friend—loyal to the point of death.

Now count your points. A score of 29–35 suggests you are well on your way to being a true friend of God; 22–28 means you'd like to be a good friend but need some work; 14–21 means you probably didn't realize you were supposed to be God's friend; 7–13 means you just don't care. (Note: If you scored low, you may find your human relationships are suffering as well. How we express our love for God directly affects our love for people—and vice versa.)

3. All through the Bible we read of an emotional God who longs to know us
   and be known by us. According to the following scriptures, what kind of
   response or emotion does God feel toward us?

   Isaiah 63:9

   Jeremiah 32:41

   Zephaniah 3:17

   How do you respond to the idea that God longs to know us and be known by
   us? Do you find that possibility comforting or frightening?

4. Write out Jeremiah 24:7 below:

5. Consider the story of the Fall found in Genesis 3:1–24. What do you think God felt when Adam and Eve chose to disobey? If He had penned a journal entry that long-ago day, what might it have said?

6. Keeping in mind the two Greek definitions for *friend* I give on page 43 of *Lazarus Awakening*—*hetairos* (friendship with self-interest in mind) and *philos* (friendship with other person's best in mind)—look up the following verses and draw a line to the type of friend each depicts.

Galatians 1:10
Acts 8:18–19   *Hetairos*
John 14:15
James 4:4   *Philos*
Ezekiel 33:31–32
Ephesians 6:24

7. Read Hebrews 8:10–12, which describes the New Covenant God has made with us through Jesus Christ. If we really understood and responded to His desire for fellowship, how would our perspective change toward the following?

Daily prayer and reading the Bible:

Attending church:

Obedience to God:

Thought life:

8. The statements below describe three famous friends of God in the Bible: Abraham, Moses, and David. Using Numbers 12:7–8; Acts 13:22; and James 2:21–23 as references, write in the space provided the name of the friend that matches the characteristic listed.

_____ He was a man after God's own heart.

_____ He was faithful in all God's house.

_____ His faith and actions worked together.

_____ He would do everything God wanted him to do.

_____ He believed God, and it was credited as righteousness.

_____ God spoke clearly to him and not in riddles.

Which, if any, of these is true of you, even in a small way?

Which of these qualities would you love to be true in your life, and why?

9. Read the following verse out loud several times, then respond to the questions that follow.

Friendship with God is reserved for those who reverence him. With them alone he shares the secrets of his promises. (Psalm 25:14, TLB)

What does this promise mean to you?

Rewrite this verse in your own words. Allow its truth to sink deep into your spirit.

10. Consider the "Help Me Love You More!" sidebar on the next page. Ask the Holy Spirit to reveal any tendencies toward friendship with the world rather than friendship with God. Fill in the following blank:

Lord, I've been lukewarm; I've chosen _____

_____

_____ **over You time and again.**

Now, write out a prayer to the Lord, asking Him to increase your ability to love Him better and more.

Help Me Love You More!

In his book *Crazy Love,* Francis Chan invites us to invite God to help us love Him more.

> If you merely pretend that you enjoy God or love Him, He knows. You can't fool Him; don't even try.
>
> Instead, tell Him how you feel. Tell Him that He isn't the most important thing in this life to you, and that you're sorry for that. Tell Him that you've been lukewarm, that you've chosen _____ over Him time and again. Tell Him that you want Him to change you, that you long to genuinely enjoy Him. Tell Him how you want to experience true satisfaction and pleasure and joy in your relationship with Him. Tell Him you want to love Him more than anything on this earth. Tell Him you want to treasure the kingdom of heaven so much that you'd willingly sell everything in order to get it. Tell Him what you like about Him, what you appreciate, and what brings you joy.
>
> *Jesus, I need to give myself up. I am not strong enough to love You and walk with You on my own. I can't do it, and I need You. I need You deeply and desperately. I believe You are worth it, that You are better than anything else I could have in this life or the next. I want You. And when I don't, I want to want You. Be all in me. Take all of me. Have Your way with me.*[10]

My heart says of you, "Seek his face!"
Your face, LORD, I will seek.

PSALM 27:8

Make a Plan

Consider your responses to question 2, "What Kind of Friend Am I?" What two things could you do this week to strengthen the weak areas you noted under the following categories:

Friendship with God

1.

2.

Friendship with Others

1.

2.

What will you do first?

Who I Am in Christ ...

Choose one of the statements from the "Who I Am in Christ" sidebar on pages 20–21 to meditate on. Write out the statement and the words of the accompanying verse. Work through the questions, then respond to God in prayer concerning the truth you've discovered.

Statement:

Verse:

What lie keeps you from accepting this as truth?

What does God's Word say about that?

Prayer:

Session Three Video
Friendship with God

I no longer call you servants, because a servant does not know his master's business. Instead, I have called you friends.

JOHN 15:15

Our Friend Lazarus, John 11:11

When Jesus referred to Lazarus, He called him "our friend." It's a term not given to many individuals, yet it is extended to us (John 15:15).

Are you a friend of God or just an acquaintance?
- Saul's relationship: "The LORD _____ God" (1 Samuel 15:15).
- David's relationship: "_____ God is my rock" (2 Samuel 22:2–3).

True Friendship with God, Psalm 25:14, *TLB*

Friendship with God doesn't happen overnight. It has to be nurtured and culti-vated. From the life of David (though not perfect), we learn that true friendship with God is:

1. Developed in _____ (Psalm 23:1–3)

2. Forged by _____ (1 Samuel 24:6)

3. Revealed by _____ on God (1 Samuel 30:6)

4. Expressed by pointing _____ to God (1 Samuel 23:16)

Closing Time

I sense the Lord saying . . .

Prayer Requests

This Week's Assignment

- Follow through with your week 3 "Make a Plan" homework.
- Read chapter 4 in *Lazarus Awakening*.
- Answer week 4 study questions.
- Continue reviewing your verses. Memorize **Jeremiah 29:11**: "'For I know the plans I have for you,' declares the LORD, 'plans to prosper you and not to harm you, plans to give you hope and a future.'"

When Love Tarries

Jesus loved Martha and her sister and Lazarus. Yet when he heard that
Lazarus was sick, he stayed where he was two more days.

JOHN 11:5–6

READ: Chapter 4 in *Lazarus Awakening*

Waiting can be the most difficult work we do. Especially when it involves waiting on the Lord.

As I said in chapter 4 of *Lazarus Awakening,* God is rarely in a hurry. Though we wish it were possible to speed things up, resurrections take time. For there are things God wants to work in us that can only be done in the dark—a transformative work that requires us to faithfully persevere over an extended period of time.

"The LORD is good to those whose hope is in him, to the one who seeks him," Lamentations 3:25–26 tells us. "It is good to wait quietly for the salvation of the LORD."

If you are currently in a waiting season, my friend, don't lose heart. Put your hope in God. Nothing is wasted in His economy. The difficulties and impossibilities you currently face provide God the material needed to perform His most masterful work.

Even when Jesus seems to tarry, never forget that you are loved. You are deeply and completely cherished by God, just as Mary and Martha were loved, though their brother had died and all hope seemed gone.

Memory Verse

"For I know the plans I have for you," declares the LORD, "plans to prosper you and not to harm you, plans to give you hope and a future."

JEREMIAH 29:11

ISRAEL MOMENT: *Jesus, the Ministry*

When I first saw Israel, I was struck by the sheer topography of this amazing land. Traveling on foot hundreds of miles in all types of conditions, Jesus went out of His way to meet ordinary people, telling them that they were loved by God. Here are some thoughts from a conversation Amy Turnage and I had concerning the ministry of Jesus.

What was travel like for Jesus?
The route from Galilee to Jerusalem took several days of walking. Through Samaria it took three days; the longest route took six. Travel was dangerous and physically demanding, yet Jesus went back and forth constantly in His ministry.

How did Jesus approach ministry?
Jesus wasn't interested in popularity; He abhorred the "cult of personality." His only mission was to point people to His Father. Jesus wasn't interested in building a following; He wanted to build followers.

Why did Jesus choose the men He did to be His disciples?
They came from all parts of society. Fishermen as well as tax collectors—they all worked hard. Judaism was inherently skeptical of professional academics; therefore, sages and disciples often had other careers as they studied the Torah.

How did Jesus "disciple" His disciples?
Jesus's brand of discipleship wasn't a once-a-week event; it was 24/7—all day, every day. That intense discipleship changed the men's lives. Even their critics "took note that these men had been with Jesus" (Acts 4:13).

What is your favorite thing about Jesus?
In so many ways, Jesus showed that He genuinely loved people. But it's His life and brilliance that inspire me. The way Jesus interacted with those He met teaches us how we should interact and love the people God brings our way.

THIS WEEK'S STUDY

1. Read John 11:1–6. Describe a time in your life when waiting was especially difficult. How did you react to the process, and what did you learn?

2. Delayed gratification is difficult for all of us. Consider the following aspects, and identify which one (or ones) you struggled with the most while growing up. Which is hardest for you today?

   • Adapting to less-than-perfect situations

   • Waiting for the fulfillment of your needs or desires

   • Accepting not only delays but also denials of what you want

   • Other:

   If possible, give specific examples:

3. One of the hardest things for many people to understand about God is that He doesn't always interrupt or intervene when we're in trouble. Instead, He specializes in redeeming the situation, using it for our good and His kingdom. Look at the following passages and write down the problem God allowed and the benefit that eventually resulted.

Situation #1

Acts 7:59–8:3   PROBLEM:

Acts 8:4; 11:19–21   RESULT:

Situation #2

Acts 21:30–36   PROBLEM:

Philippians 1:12–14   RESULT:

4. We humans tend to love formulas, thinking that if we do certain things, then God will have to do the things we've asked Him to do. We often think that our A+B should always result in God doing C. What do the following verses say about God's sovereign wisdom?

Isaiah 55:8–9

Romans 11:33–34

Pause a moment and allow this heavenly perspective to sink into your heart. Write a response to the Lord concerning the ways you've tried to control Him through "formulas" rather than simply trusting He knows what is best.

5. Read "The Blessing of Trouble" sidebar on the next page. How have you experienced the benefits of hardship in your life?

The Blessing of Trouble

Of all the hard sayings of the Bible, perhaps none is as difficult to understand as Jesus's response to Lazarus's death in John 11:15. "For your sake I am glad I was not there," He tells the disciples. But then He adds the reason: "so that you may believe." Jesus knows that some of life's greatest gifts come wrapped in disappointments, and faith is often learned best in the crucible of pain. Listen to Charles Haddon Spurgeon's thoughts on this verse:

> If you want to ruin your son, never let him know a hardship. When he is a child carry him in your arms, when he becomes a youth still dandle him, and when he becomes a man still dry-nurse him, and you will succeed in producing an arrant fool. If you want to prevent his being made useful in the world, guard him from every kind of toil. Do not suffer him to struggle. Wipe the sweat from his dainty brow and say, "Dear child, thou shalt never have another task so arduous." Pity him when he ought to be punished; supply all his wishes, avert all disappointments, prevent all troubles, and you will surely tutor him to be a reprobate and to break your heart. But put him where he must work, expose him to difficulties, purposely throw him into peril, and in this way you shall make him a man, and when he comes to do man's work and to bear man's trial, he shall be fit for either. My Master does not daintily cradle His children when they ought to run alone; and when they begin to run He is not always putting out His finger for them to lean upon, but He lets them tumble down to the cutting of their knees, because then they will walk more carefully by-and-by, and learn to stand upright by the strength which faith confers upon them.
>
> You see, dear friends, that Jesus Christ was glad—glad that His disciples were blessed by trouble. Will you think of this, you who are so troubled this morning, Jesus Christ does sympathize with you, but still He does it wisely, and He says, "I am glad for your sakes that I was not there."[11]

6. Read Psalm 40:1–5, then list five benefits of waiting patiently for the Lord. Circle the benefit that means the most to you.

-

-

-

-

-

7. What do the following verses say about the difficulties we face in this life?

Genesis 50:20

John 16:33

1 Peter 4:12–14

8. Read the following statements, made by Pastor Don Burleson, and circle the truth that you need most today.

- God is *love*—therefore I am loved.

- God is *good*—therefore I am safe.

- God is *faithful*—therefore it's going to be okay. For God is incapable of doing anything less than marvelous things.[12]

Why did you choose that one?

How would your life be different if you could get these three truths from your head to your heart?

9. Read the story of the blind man in John 9:1–7. When you're trying to figure out why things have gone wrong in your life, who or what are you tempted to blame?

Write out Jesus's response in John 9:3:

10. Now read aloud the New Living Translation of John 11:4, but replace
Lazarus's name with yours:

**But when Jesus heard about it he said, "_____'s sickness will
not end in death. No, it happened for the glory of God so that the Son of
God will receive glory from this."**

Consider John 11:4 as you read John 9:3 once again. What do these verses
mean to you in your current situation? If you'd like, write your response in
the form of a prayer.

Make a Plan

In what area of your life do you feel God calling you to hand Him the "quill of your will" as Martha did in John 11:21–22?

Which of the three points listed in "The Art of Waiting" sidebar on the next page do you need to apply to this situation?

List two practical ways you could begin to do that this week:

1.

2.

Write down any breakthroughs you experience:

The Art of Waiting

Have you ever felt the need to rush ahead of God? All through Scripture we are encouraged to develop the all-important—and really difficult—art of waiting. Warren Wiersbe shares three statements in Scripture that have helped him hone prayerful patience in his own life—principles he applies whenever he feels nervous about a situation and is tempted to hurry God:

1. "**Stand still**, and see the salvation of the LORD" (Exodus 14:13, NKJV).

2. "**Sit still** . . . until you know how the matter will turn out" (Ruth 3:18, NKJV).

3. "**Be still**, and know that I am God" (Psalm 46:10, NKJV).

"When you wait on the Lord in prayer," Wiersbe writes, "you are not wasting your time; you are investing it. God is preparing both you and your circumstances so that His purposes will be accomplished. However, when the right time arrives for us to act by faith, we dare not delay."[13]

But they that wait upon the LORD shall renew their strength;
they shall mount up with wings as eagles; they shall run,
and not be weary; and they shall walk, and not faint.

ISAIAH 40:31, KJV

Who I Am in Christ ...

Choose one of the statements from the "Who I Am in Christ" sidebar on pages 20–21 to meditate on. Write out the statement and the words of the accompanying verse. Work through the questions, then respond to God in prayer concerning the truth you've discovered.

Statement:

Verse:

What lie keeps you from accepting this as truth?

What does God's Word say about that?

Prayer:

Session Four Video

Shaped in the Quarry

And in him you too are being built together to become a dwelling in which God lives by his Spirit.

EPHESIANS 2:22

Created to Be God's Dwelling, 2 Corinthians 6:16

God doesn't "dwell in temples" made by human hands (Acts 17:24, NKJV), but in you and me.

We are meant to be "living stones" (1 Peter 2:5).
- The temple stones were shaped in the quarry (1 Kings 6:7).
- God does some of His best work in the _____.

Building a Temple

In order to become living stones worthy of God's temple, we must be:

1. _____ in secret

2. _____ to His touch

3. Honed to fit with _____

4. Made ready _____ and out

It All Begins at the Altar, Joshua 8:31 and Romans 12:1

As we offer our lives to God—as imperfect as they are!—He uses them to build a temple to display His glory to the world.

Closing Time

I sense the Lord saying . . .

Prayer Requests

This Week's Assignment

- Follow through with your week 4 "Make a Plan" homework.
- Read chapters 5 and 6 in *Lazarus Awakening.*
- Answer week 5 study questions.
- Plan to start early on your week 5 "Make a Plan" homework as there are daily assignments.
- Continue reviewing your verses. Memorize **John 11:40:** "Then Jesus said, 'Did I not tell you that if you believed, you would see the glory of God?'"

Tomb Dwelling

"Where have you laid him?" he asked. "Come and see, Lord," they replied. Jesus wept.

JOHN 11:34–35

READ: Chapters 5 and 6 in *Lazarus Awakening*

Have you ever felt stuck? Unable to move or escape a tight spot?

It's amazing how often we settle for living in small spaces in our souls. How often we choose the cramped corners of self-preservation rather than the wide-open spaces of God's provision and care. The confining limitations we place on ourselves—out of fear or simply the unwillingness to take a risk—hold us back in more ways than we know.

Tombs come in all shapes and sizes. Some we craft ourselves. Some have been created by others. But none of them can hold us captive if we'll call out to Jesus. For the same power that "raised Jesus from the dead," Romans 8:11 tells us, "will also give life to your mortal bodies through his Spirit, who lives in you."

It is an "incomparably great power," Ephesians 1:19 tells us, and it's the power the Holy Spirit wants to use on our behalf. Shattering strongholds and helping us roll away stones. Bringing us out of our tombs and into new life.

If we will give God permission to invade every dark corner of our hearts, He will bring the freedom each one of us needs.

Memory Verse

Then Jesus said, "Did I not tell you that if you believed, you would see the glory of God?"

JOHN 11:40

ISRAEL MOMENT: *Archaeology and the Bible*

Everywhere you go in this beautiful land, you come across meaningful spots and important finds that have been uncovered by archaeologists. In this "Israel Moment," Israel expert and my friend Amy Turnage talks about several of those discoveries.

Pottery and Coins: As archaeologists dig down through layers of dirt and rubble, they date the layers by using coins and shards of pottery found in the excavation. Coin markings as well as shapes and thicknesses of pottery help identify the time period.

Tel Dan Inscription: Thirty years ago, some scholars began to believe David may have been a mythical figure like King Arthur. In 1990, at the city of Dan, the first extrabiblical mention of David and his dynasty in Judah were found on fragments of monumental inscription dated to the ninth century BC.[14] A subsequent reading of the Mesha Stele (known as the Moabite Stone) revealed a mention of the House of David as well.[15]

Dedication of Temple to Tiberias: This inscription provides an important window into the psychology of Pontius Pilate. We know from ancient sources that Pilate was a brutal man, yet he dedicated a temple to a living Roman emperor, which was very unusual.[16] No wonder Pilate was so motivated by the statement of the chief priest, "If you let this man go, you are no friend of Caesar" (John 19:12).

Biblical Locations: Archaeology helps to discover and confirm actual locations mentioned in Scripture. Amy and her husband, Marc, are currently excavating a location on the Sea of Galilee that may turn out to be the site of Bethsaida, which has long been in question. You can learn more about this project at Marc's website: Theshardandthescroll.com.

They told them, "Go, explore the land."

JUDGES 18:2

THIS WEEK'S STUDY

1. Read the section in chapter 5 titled "Caught Between Death and Life" (pages 69 and 71 in *Lazarus Awakening*). What are some indications that we may be stuck in midchamber living?

2. Consider the "Hurts, Hang-Ups, and Habits" sidebar on page 70 in *Lazarus Awakening.* Which of these three categories of strongholds tends to keep you from moving forward in your walk with God?

   Name at least one item you struggle with in that area (or have given in to).

   Listen to God's heart toward His people in Psalm 107:20:

   He sent His word and healed them, and delivered them from their destructions. (NKJV)

   What does this example of God's merciful compassion mean to you?

3. We all have lies that we've internalized as truth, unhealthy patterns that undermine the life God wants us to live. To help you discover what might be holding you back from freedom, ask the Holy Spirit to lead you as you read Appendix E: "Identifying Strongholds" in *Lazarus Awakening* (softcover, pages 223–25; hardcover pages 203–5). As you read each point, answer the corresponding question below as honestly as you can.

Do you struggle with "repeated, unwanted behavior"?

Do you tend to turn to this behavior or thought pattern when things are difficult or you feel depressed?

Do you have difficulty understanding why you react to certain things the way you do?

Do you have a secret no one knows?

Do you find yourself stuck somewhere in your past or stalled in the grief process?

Do you have an unsubstantiated and intense dislike of a certain type or group of people?

Do you accept your limitations as your definition?

Do you get offended when other people point out unhealthy behaviors that you don't (or do!) see in yourself?

4. Using the "Dethroning Lies" sidebar on page 59, work through anything you discovered in question 3. Write a short prayer for each step.

REVEAL:

REPENT:

RENOUNCE:

REPLACE:

5. The book of Isaiah gives us a glimpse into the many purposes of Jesus's coming and ministry. List the things you discover concerning those purposes in Isaiah 61:1–3.

Dethroning Lies

Many of us believe the lie that we are helpless when it comes to finding true freedom. Our bondage seems too strong and the lies too intense. Yet regularly employing these four powerful principles releases the Holy Spirit to release us:

Reveal. Ask God to show the area (or areas) in which you are bound. What stronghold is holding you back from freedom? What lie has exalted itself above the knowledge of God? Don't try to figure this out on your own. Ask for the Spirit's help.

Repent. Ask God to forgive the times you've sought refuge in your stronghold rather than in Him. Ask the Holy Spirit to take your sin and the accompanying lies and remove them from you "as far as the east is from the west" (Psalm 103:12).

Renounce. Prayerfully renounce any authority you may have given to Satan when you embraced your stronghold rather than God. Naming each sin aloud, renounce your attachment to the lie or behavior, giving authority in that area back to Jesus Christ.

Replace. Look for scriptures that pertain to your stronghold or the lie you've believed. Write down these verses and place them where you can read them several times a day. Memorize and quote these verses whenever you feel the lie trying to reassert its power.

Please note that I'm not outlining four easy steps for curing your hurts, hang-ups, and habits. Strongholds may have a physical or spiritual component, so the process of breaking free can be lengthy and complicated. Some (especially addictions) may require significant time to overcome as well as outside help, such as professional counseling, support groups, intercessory prayer, and more.

The weapons we fight with are not the weapons of the world.
On the contrary, they have divine power to demolish strongholds.

2 CORINTHIANS 10:4

6. Unfortunately, many of us tend to be *Christian atheists,* as Craig Groeschel puts it, "believing in God but living as if He doesn't exist."[17] Give an example (big or little) of this contradiction in your own life or in the lives of Christians in general.

What could we do to better fight the tendency toward Christian atheism?

7. God went out of His way to remove the barrier that stood between us and Him, both physically and spiritually. Look up the following passages and describe how He accomplished this. (I've started the first one for you.)

Leviticus 16:2   THE BARRIER: *The curtain (or veil) in the temple*

Matthew 27:50–51   THE PROCESS:

Hebrews 10:19–22   THE RESULT:

8. Which one of the following "stones" might be blocking God's access to the places in you that need healing? Look up the corresponding verses and write down favorite words or phrases that speak most to you. Ask God to help you remove anything standing in the way of your freedom.

Unworthiness (Romans 4:7–8; 8:1)

Unforgiveness (Ephesians 4:31–32; 5:1–2)

Unbelief (Romans 4:18–22)

Make note of any other stones—besides these three—that might be keeping you from Him.

9. Rolling away stones and leaving our tombs can be a scary process. Read the words of Jesus below.

> Did I not tell you that if you believed, you would see the glory of God? (John 11:40)

As you hear Jesus asking you to roll away whatever might be blocking your heart, what does His response to Martha mean to you?

10. Using the words of the desperate father in Mark 9:24 as a template—"I do believe; help me overcome my unbelief!"—write a prayer asking God to increase your faith.

Make a Plan

In order to leave our tombs behind, we need to change the way we think. Each day this week, we're going to work on one of the points listed in the "Disciplining Your Mind" sidebar on pages 65–66. Read the description carefully, looking up any listed verses, then come up with an action step to take that day. Later, record any victories you experienced.

DAY ONE: *Take every thought captive.*

Action Step:

Victory:

DAY TWO: *Resist vain imaginations.*

Action Step:

Victory:

DAY THREE: *Refuse to agree with the devil.*

Action Step:

Victory:

DAY FOUR: *Bless those who curse you.*

Action Step:

Victory:

DAY FIVE: *Renew your mind with the Word of God.*

Action Step:

Victory:

DAY SIX: *Speak truth to yourself.*

Action Step:

Victory:

DAY SEVEN: *Develop an attitude of gratitude.*

Action Step:

Victory:

Disciplining Your Mind

"The battlefield is the mind" when it comes to the enemy's attempt to derail our Christianity. But the best defense has always been a good offense, so I'm learning to train my mind for battle by practicing the following disciplines:

1. *Take every thought captive* (2 Corinthians 10:5). Or, as Joyce Meyer puts it, "Think about what you are thinking about."[18] Try not to let your mind wander indiscriminately. Instead, consider where your thoughts could lead you. If the thought takes you away from God, cut it off. (You really can do this!) Consciously bring your mind back to Jesus and leave it there.

2. *Resist vain imaginations* (Romans 1:21, KJV)—you know, those runaway loops of what-ifs, if onlys, and woulda-coulda-shouldas. When you feel yourself getting caught up in a cycle of fear, worry, or regret, stop! Consciously rein in your imagination, and shift your focus to Christ as the source of your peace (Isaiah 26:3).

3. *Refuse to agree with the devil.* When thoughts of condemnation or fear come to mind, remind yourself that they are lies, that God is bigger than your biggest problem and stronger than your greatest weakness (Philippians 4:13), and that He's taken care of the Accuser's accusations once and for all (Revelation 12:10–11).

4. *Bless those who curse you* (Luke 6:28). If you carry a grudge in your heart, it will consume your mind. When resentment arises against someone, begin praying *for*, not *against*, that person. Ask God to bless and reveal Himself to him or her . . . and to help you move past your resentment. (It may take some time to actually *feel* forgiving!)

5. *Renew your mind with the Word of God* (Romans 12:2; Ephesians 5:26). Get into the Word daily, and allow it to transform your thinking. Find a scripture that speaks to your particular situation, then memorize it, making it part of your mental arsenal against the lies of the enemy.

6. *Speak truth to yourself* (John 8:32). Too many of us play and replay demeaning self-talk and other negative ideas that are contrary to what God has said. Consciously counter that tendency by repeating God's truth to yourself. Declare what you know to be greater than what you feel, proclaiming what God says about you and His power to save.

7. *Develop an attitude of gratitude.* Purposefully think about things that are of "good report" (Philippians 4:8, KJV). Make a list if you need to. Don't give voice to negativity—inwardly or outwardly. Instead, declare out loud your thankfulness to God (1 Thessalonians 5:18).

> *And now, dear brothers and sisters, one final thing. Fix your thoughts on what is true, and honorable, and right, and pure, and lovely, and admirable. Think about things that are excellent and worthy of praise.*
>
> PHILIPPIANS 4:8, NLT

Who I Am in Christ ...

Choose one of the statements from the "Who I Am in Christ" sidebar on pages 20–21 to meditate on. Write out the statement and the words of the accompanying verse. Work through the questions, then respond to God in prayer concerning the truth you've discovered.

Statement:

Verse:

What lie keeps you from accepting this as truth?

What does God's Word say about that?

Prayer:

Leaving Our Tombs

I pray also that the eyes of your heart may be enlightened in order that you may know the hope to which he has called you, the riches of his glorious inheritance in the saints, and his incomparably great power for us who believe.

EPHESIANS 1:18–19

We Serve a Mighty God, Ephesians 1:17–20

We need to realize the mighty power of God working on our behalf. But while we serve a mighty God, we also have a formidable foe (1 Peter 5:8).

Satan seeks to:

- Hem us in
- Shut us down
- Close us off

The Dark Plot

Satan desires to keep us from being effective in God's kingdom. He wants to:

1. Marginalize us

2. _____ us

3. _____ us

The Glorious Answer, Psalm 40:1–3, NLT

Jesus wants to set us free from our tombs so that He can open us up to be all He intends us to be . . .

A _____ case for His splendor!

Notes

Closing Time

I sense the Lord saying . . .

Prayer Requests

This Week's Assignment

- Follow through with your week 5 "Make a Plan" homework.
- Read chapter 7 in *Lazarus Awakening*.
- Answer week 6 study questions.
- Plan to start early on your week 6 "Make a Plan" homework as you'll be doing it throughout the week.
- Continue to review your verses. Memorize **Romans 5:8:** "But God demonstrates his own love for us in this: While we were still sinners, Christ died for us."

When Love Calls Your Name

When he had said this, Jesus called in a loud voice, "Lazarus, come out!"
The dead man came out, his hands and feet wrapped with strips of linen,
and a cloth around his face.

JOHN 11:43–44

READ: Chapter 7 in *Lazarus Awakening*

A name is a powerful thing. When we hear ours called by a familiar voice, the noise around us can't drown it out. For we've been recognized. Noticed and acknowledged in the midst of a crowd. Valued and set apart.

I wonder how different our lives would be if we understood how significant we are to God. That the same One who created the stars and "calls them each by name" (Psalm 147:4) knows us intimately as well. That His thoughts toward us "outnumber the grains of sand" (Psalm 139:18). There is nothing about us that escapes God's notice, nor His tender care.

You are beloved by your heavenly Father, my friend. No matter what you've done or where you've been, the Lord says: "I have redeemed you; I have summoned you by name; you are mine" (Isaiah 43:1).

So when you sense Jesus calling your name, don't shrink back! You aren't being singled out for punishment or as an object of His wrath. No, no, no. Far from that, Jesus calls your name because He loves you and wants to make you His very own.

Memory Verse

But God demonstrates his own love for us in this: While we were still sinners, Christ died for us.

ROMANS 5:8

ISRAEL MOMENT: *Drinking the Cup*

The night Jesus prayed in the Garden of Gethsemane was a crucible night in the life of our Savior (Matthew 26:36–56). A night—and a decision—that would change the world. Amy Turnage and I discuss this dark moment.

What do you think Gethsemane was like for Jesus?
We need to remember that Jesus was fully human and fully God. He had to experience the same things we experience—the feelings and the fear of what was about to happen. Jesus made a costly choice that night. And in His example, we learn how to respond when faced with our own "Gethsemane."

Did Jesus have other options?
Yes, He did. Jesus didn't have to surrender when the soldiers came to arrest Him (John 18:4–6). He could have easily escaped over the Mount of Olives and quickly been lost in the desert. Staying wasn't an easy decision (Matthew 26:39). But instead of choosing to run, Jesus chose to be obedient to His Father.

What does Gethsemane mean to you?
Gethsemane means that when things are difficult, when there are hard choices to make, I need to give that part of my life to God. I need to be willing to do the hard thing, even when it's painful and involves suffering. When we are obedient, there is a peace and a strength that helps us do God's will. When we refuse, there is turmoil.

The name Gethsemane means "oil press"; do you think that's significant?
The work of an oil press was important for Jewish life and worship. Olives would be pressed in it to provide oil for three uses:
- First pressing for the Temple
- Second pressing for cosmetics and food
- Third pressing for lamp oil

God wants to use the "Gethsemane" pressing times in our lives as well—for His glory and for our transformation—so that we can each become a light to the world.

This Week's Study

1. Did you have a nickname growing up? What did your mom call you when you were in trouble, and how did you respond?

2. If you were administered a spiritual hearing test today, what do you think the results would be? Check one answer below.

   ____ Excellent

   ____ Improving

   ____ Average

   ____ Poor

   ____ Acute deafness

   What do you normally do when you have difficulty hearing someone?

   What one thing could you do to raise your level of spiritual hearing?

3. Read the following passage from Priscilla Shirer's book *Discerning the Voice of God:*

> If God wants us to hear His voice, the Father of Lies is going to do everything he can to make us think that we *aren't* hearing it. When we hear from God, we call it intuition, coincidence, or even luck—anything but what it is: the voice of God. We're so used to dismissing His voice that we've convinced ourselves that He no longer speaks to His children. But the Bible says over and over that God *does* speak to us. We *are* hearing from Him. We just may not know it's Him.[19]

What lies has the enemy used to try to convince you that you can't or don't hear God's voice?

How does it make you feel to think that God wants to communicate with you?

4. Read about Elijah's encounter with God in 1 Kings 19:11–12, then write out Isaiah 30:21 below.

What do these two passages of Scripture reveal about the ways God tends to speak to us today?

5. Describe a time God spoke to you in a "whisper" or as the "voice behind you." What did He speak to your heart, and how did you know it was Him?

6. Part of hearing God's voice involves listening to what He has already said in His Word, but true listening requires obedience. Beneath each reference, list the benefits that come when we hear God's Word and apply it to our lives:

Proverbs 4:10–13

James 1:22–25

7. Write out the following verses:

Acts 22:14

Mark 4:24–25

Now, go back and underline or circle key words or phrases. What stood out most to you?

8. Mark each of the following descriptions concerning the Holy Spirit's work in our lives with the letter of the corresponding verse: (a) John 14:26; (b) John 16:13–15; (c) 1 Corinthians 2:12–14.

____ Gives us spiritual discernment

____ Teaches us all things

____ Guides us into all truth

____ Helps us understand what God has given us

____ Brings glory to Christ by revealing to us what belongs to Him

____ Reminds us of everything Jesus has said

____ Tells us what is to come

____ Gives us the words to express spiritual truths

9. On the next page, read the story of Jesus and the three praying women. (See the complete story on pages 116–17 in *Lazarus Awakening*.) What speaks most to you from this story?

10. God is the same God today as He has always been. Though it might not be in an audible voice, He wants to speak to you and me just as He spoke to His people throughout the Bible. Read 1 Samuel 3:1–21. Now consider the following quote from Oswald Chambers:

God [often speaks to us] in ways that are easy to misunderstand, and we say, "I wonder if that is God's voice?" Isaiah said that the Lord spake to him "with a strong hand," that is, by the pressure of circumstances. Nothing touches our lives but it is God Himself speaking. Do we discern His hand or only mere occurrence?

   Get into the habit of saying, "Speak, Lord," and life will become a romance. [20]

Respond to what you sense the Holy Spirit speaking to your heart by writing a prayer, starting with these words:

Speak, Lord . . .

When Love Seems Silent

I've found comfort in a little story I once read—a story about a woman who dreamed she saw three people praying. She watched Jesus draw near and approach the first figure, leaning over her tenderly. Then He proceeded to the next figure, placing a gentle hand on her head and nodding with "loving approval." But what happened next perplexed the dreaming woman:

The third woman He passed almost abruptly without stopping for a word or glance. The woman in her dream said to herself, "How greatly He must love the first one, to the second He gave His approval, . . . and the third must have grieved Him deeply, for He gave her no word at all and not even a passing look." . . .

As she tried to account for the action of her Lord, He Himself stood by her and said: "O woman! how wrongly hast thou interpreted Me. The first kneeling woman needs all the weight of My tenderness and care to keep her feet in My narrow way. She needs My love, thought and help every moment of the day. Without it she would fail and fall.

"The second has stronger faith and deeper love, and I can trust her to trust Me however things may go and whatever people do.

"The third, whom I seemed not to notice, and even to neglect, has faith and love of the finest quality, and her I am training by quick and drastic processes for the highest and holiest service.

"She knows Me so intimately, and trusts Me so utterly, that she is independent of words or looks or any outward intimation of My approval. . . . because she knows that I am working in her for eternity, and that what I do, though she knows not the explanation now, she will understand hereafter."[21]

Dear friend, don't be afraid of the times when Christ seems "silent in his love" (Zephaniah 3:17, DRA), when He answers "not a word" (Matthew 15:23, KJV). Because God is up to something more in your life and mine than just giving us the comfort of His voice.

Make a Plan

Read over the "Tuning Our Hearts" sidebar on the next page. (For the complete text, go to pages 112–13 in *Lazarus Awakening*.) Throughout the week, keep your ears tuned to the different ways God might choose to speak to you. Record them in the space below. Also note past occasions when God used one or more of these methods. (Remember, often it isn't until after we've obeyed that we realize that it was God's voice speaking all along!)

REPEATED THEMES:

IMPRESSIONS:

CONFIRMATIONS:

CHECKS:

OTHER:

What did you learn through this exercise?

Tuning Our Hearts by Recognizing His Ways

While Scripture is the main way God speaks to me, it's not the only way. In fact, I've been amazed at His creativity and the variety of experiences He uses to communicate with me. Here are four methods the Spirit seems to use often:

- *Repeated themes.* Like every wise parent, God repeats Himself when we don't listen the first time![22] So I've learned to be on the lookout for similar messages on similar topics coming from different sources. If the same topic keeps coming up, God is usually trying to tell me something.

- *Impressions.* This wisdom from the Spirit usually involves an inner urge or prodding to do something or to go in a certain direction. Sometimes it's very specific, but to be honest, it's often tricky to tell whether the impulse is God's idea or my own. After I obey the nudge, however, I can often look back and see it really was from God.

- *Confirmations.* This clarification from the Holy Spirit is especially important when I'm uncertain whether I'm hearing God correctly. Sometimes corroboration comes through Scripture or from other people, but it can also come from a sense of settled peace.

- *Checks.* Sometimes instead of confirmation I may feel a check regarding certain decisions or actions. There may be nothing obviously wrong with the action I'm contemplating, nothing that bothers my conscience, but I don't have peace about it. Later I may (or may not) come to understand what the Spirit was warning against, but that isn't as important as the fact that I've obeyed.

Regardless of which of these methods God uses to speak to us, it's important to remember that He will never go against His Word. Therefore, if any communication fails to measure up with the Bible, I must set it aside, no matter how genuinely I believe I've heard from God. That is why it is so important that we know the Word.

Who I Am in Christ ...

Choose one of the statements from the "Who I Am in Christ" sidebar on pages 20–21 to meditate on. Write out the statement and the words of the accompanying verse. Work through the questions, then respond to God in prayer concerning the truth you've discovered.

Statement:

Verse:

What lie keeps you from accepting this as truth?

What does God's Word say about that?

Prayer:

Session Six Video

Do You Want to Be Well?

*Now there is in Jerusalem near the Sheep Gate a pool, which in Aramaic
is called Bethesda. . . . Here a great number of disabled people used to
lie—the blind, the lame, the paralyzed.*

JOHN 5:2–3

A Man with a Problem, John 5:1–14

Jesus encountered a man who had suffered for thirty-eight years, longer than many
people lived at that time.

The question: "Do you want to get well?" (verse 6)
The response: Fixated on his _____ rather than his Savior (verse 7)

Steps to Wholeness

Like the man, if we want to be healed, we must:

1. Stop making _____.

2. Look to the right _____.

3. Take a leap of _____.

4. Leave old life behind.

5. Stop _____.

Notes

Closing Time

I sense the Lord saying . . .

Prayer Requests

This Week's Assignment

- Follow through with your week 6 "Make a Plan" homework.
- Read chapters 8 and 11 (bonus chapter in the softcover edition) in
  Lazarus Awakening. For those with a hardcover edition, the bonus
  chapter 11 is available for download at LazarusAwakening.com.
- Answer week 7 study questions.
- Continue to review your verses. Memorize **Galatians 5:1:** "It is for
  freedom that Christ has set us free. Stand firm, then, and do not let
  yourselves be burdened again by a yoke of slavery."

Unwinding Graveclothes

Jesus said to them, "Take off the grave clothes and let him go."

JOHN 11:44

READ: Chapters 8 and 11 (bonus chapter) in *Lazarus Awakening*

*I*t's a messy process, loving people back to life. The residue of death and the unhealthy patterns of graveclothes cling to us all, even seasoned Christians. They make us trip and stumble at times, fumble and bumble—not to mention, grumble. Despite our incompleteness, God has chosen us to come alongside others who also struggle to leave their tombs behind.

Sanctification—that is, becoming more like Jesus—is a process, not an event. Realizing that has helped me so much in my walk with God and in my relationships with people. When I'm reminded of Christ's patience with me and my continual need of His grace and forgiveness, I'm quicker to extend grace and forgiveness to others.

Rather than looking down on one another, together we are enabled to look up, to the One—the only One—who can save us. As we each unwind our own graveclothes through repentance and obedience, we begin to shed the unhealthy patterns and dark lies that have bound us far too long.

Then, with the Holy Spirit's help, we leave our tombs behind and walk out into new life, just as Lazarus did. Unbound and unhindered. Sanctified and set free.

Memory Verse

It is for freedom that Christ has set us free. Stand firm, then, and do not let yourselves be burdened again by a yoke of slavery.

GALATIANS 5:1

ISRAEL MOMENT: *Embracing the Cross*

It was on a road like the Via Dolorosa that Jesus carried His cross as He made His way to Calvary (John 19:16–18). But in a very real sense, Jesus had been walking that path since the day He was born. Amy Turnage and I talk about this important moment in history and what it means for us today.

Why crucifixion?

Crucifixion served as crowd control. Josephus, the Jewish historian, tells us the soldiers of Titus crucified so many people that "there was no room for the crosses, and no crosses for the bodies."[23] Prior to actual crucifixion, many were subjected to torture and beaten with a whip called a "cat of nine tails." This beating killed many. Those who made it to the cross most likely died from hypovolemic shock—a condition characterized by low blood pressure and reduced blood flow, leading to irreversible cell and organ injury, and eventually death.

Why did Jesus have to die?

Of course, Christ's redemptive death had been in the mind of God since the beginning of time, but the Bible tells us the religious establishment viewed Jesus as a threat to their power and economic wealth (John 11:48). They couldn't openly kill or arrest Jesus because of His popularity, so they used the cloak of darkness and a dirty deal between the high priest and Pontius Pilate to kill Jesus. Money and power corrupted people then, just as it does today.

What did Christ's death accomplish?

On the cross, Jesus took all of our shame and pain. It must have seemed like God Himself had turned away as Jesus cried out, "Why have you forsaken me?" (Matthew 27:46). In His sacrificial act, Jesus took all of our loneliness, our abandonment issues, and most important, all of our sin.

No one took Jesus's life. He gave it willingly. And because He died on the cross that long-ago day, the trajectory of our paths has been drastically altered. Heaven awaits! All because Jesus was willing to walk the Via Dolorosa.

THIS WEEK'S STUDY

1. Read the story of the Good Samaritan in Luke 10:30–37. If you had been on the road that day, which of the following roles might you have played? (I've embellished a bit.)

> *The Priest*—saw the bruised and bleeding man, but kept moving, too busy to stop.
>
> *The Levite*—looked more closely, but didn't feel adequate to help. Dialed 911 as he went on his way.
>
> *The Soccer Mom*—distracted by squabbling kids and text messages, she didn't even notice.
>
> *The Samaritan*—laid aside his plans and got involved, helping the wounded man.

2. Read the "Kissing Frogs" sidebar on page 124 of *Lazarus Awakening*. It's been said that we should love people when they least expect it and least deserve it. Describe a time when someone loved you like that—or a time when you had the privilege of doing that for someone else.

3. From the sidebar on the next page, which of the "Lessons from Good Sam" speaks most to you?

Which one seems the most challenging? Why?

Lessons from Good Sam

We all want to be used by God to help others. But we don't always know what that should look like. The story of the good Samaritan offers several lessons to help shape our response when we see someone in need:

- *He not only saw but also acted.* Other people passed by and saw the wounded man, but the good Samaritan was "moved" with compassion. He didn't just feel sorry for the man's condition; he *moved* to do something to alleviate his pain (Proverbs 3:27).
- *He used his oil and his donkey.* Don't underestimate what your involvement can mean to someone in need. Investing your practical resources, your emotional support, and your precious time can make all the difference to a broken soul. A kind note, a warm meal, a listening ear—little is much when God is in it (James 2:16; Galatians 6:2).
- *He went out of his way to help.* Initial compassion can wear off quickly, especially when helping others is inconvenient. The good Samaritan could have left the man at the inn and gone on his way, but instead he stuck around to do the hard stuff—washing wounds and staying beside him through a long, painful night (Galatians 6:9).
- *He left the man in capable hands.* There will be times when a person's needs may be beyond our ability to help—times when a pastor, a godly counselor, or another professional will be required. Connecting needy people to other resources may be the most important thing we do (Proverbs 13:10).
- *He promised to stay engaged in the process.* Following through to see how the person is doing is important—though at times God may ask us to do more. Whatever is required, never underestimate the importance of intercession—standing in the gap as Ezekiel did (Ezekiel 22:30), fighting for final victory in the lives of those we minister to.

4. Do you have a friend or acquaintance who is struggling to escape graveclothes right now? If you'd like, write that person's name or situation here:

Now, prayerfully read through the "Hints for Unwinding Graveclothes" found in Appendix F in *Lazarus Awakening* (softcover, pages 227–29; hardcover pages 207–9). Which of these points resonates most? In what way(s) do you sense God would want you to respond to this person or situation?

Note: Don't underestimate the power of a simple phone call, a shared meal, or an encouraging note. Whatever the Holy Spirit lays on your heart, do it—God wants to love that person through you.

5. While we've discussed how we can help others unwind their graveclothes, what does Hebrews 12:1–6 tell us about unwinding our own? List at least five things we should do.

-
-
-
-
-

Which of these things do you most need to do today, and why?

6. Before we can discard our graveclothes, we need to recognize them. Of the responses identified in the "Tripping Points" sidebar on page 92, which ones do you default to most often?

What types of situations seem to reveal these weak spots?

7. Read the "Shedding Graveclothes" sidebar on page 93. Look up the corresponding verses and write down the one that speaks most to you.

How could you begin applying these steps to help you form new responses? What other transformational steps come to mind?

8. Though you considered this passage earlier, I'd like to focus on it once again. Underline and highlight anything that stands out to you as you read Hebrews 12:1–3 in The Message.

Do you see what this means—all these pioneers who blazed the way, all these veterans cheering us on? It means we'd better get on with it. Strip down, start running—and never quit! No extra spiritual fat, no parasitic sins. Keep your eyes on Jesus, who both began and finished this race we're in. Study how he did it. Because he never lost sight of where he was headed—that exhilarating finish in and with God—he could put up with anything along the way: cross, shame, whatever. And now he's there, in the place of honor, right alongside God. When you find yourselves flagging in your faith, go over that story again, item by item, that long litany of hostility he plowed through. That will shoot adrenaline into your souls!

9. Using your Bible translation, write out Hebrews 12:4 below.

With Hebrews 12:1–4 in mind, especially verse 4, respond to the Lord in prayer.

Tripping Points

Graveclothes are often revealed by repeated reactions and cyclical responses. For instance, if you find yourself offended by someone, only to be offended by someone else the very next day, that's a sign that other people might not be the problem. Consider the following emotions and behaviors. (Note there is space for you to add others that come to mind.)

Are any of these responses overly familiar to you? Number the three that occur most often in you. Then prayerfully consider the "Shedding Grave-clothes" suggestions on the opposite page.

_____ insecurity	_____ need to control	_____ urge to escape
_____ negativity	_____ depression	_____ self-pity
_____ touchiness	_____ emotional "stuffing"	_____ sharp tongue
_____ self-hatred	_____ fear	_____ self-centeredness
_____ quick temper	_____ dishonesty	_____ easily offended
_____ procrastination	_____ emotional bully	_____ isolation
_____ shame	_____ defensiveness	_____ judgmentalism
_____ blame	_____ self-medicating	_____ envy
_____ fantasizing	_____ denial	_____ people pleasing
_____ self-justification	_____ resentment	_____ paranoia
_____ other:	_____ other:	_____ other:

Search me, O God, and know my heart.... See if there is any offensive way in me, and lead me in the way everlasting.

PSALM 139:23–24

Shedding Graveclothes

When it comes to getting rid of the graveclothes that trip me up, I've always wanted God to deal with me quickly, the way a chef slices an onion. But God knows what I need, and in His wisdom and mercy, He takes me at a pace I can handle. Here's the shroud-shedding process I've found helpful as I have tried to cooperate with God's work in my life.

1. Ask God to reveal the graveclothes you need to remove (Psalm 139:23–24). They may include besetting sins, lies, or cyclical patterns you identified in the previous sidebar, "Tripping Points." Ask Him to show you the truth about the danger they pose and to help you let them go.

2. Choose new responses before you find yourself in trigger situations. In many cases, this involves determining to do the opposite of what comes naturally—for instance, being quiet rather than reacting with lots of words (Romans 12:2).

3. Don't get discouraged when the process takes time. Some grave-clothes have more layers than others. The fact that a certain issue reappears doesn't negate or diminish what God has done in you. It may not be the same layer but a deeper one (2 Corinthians 3:18).

4. Multiple layers of graveclothes may indicate an area of vulnerability that you will always struggle with. Guard yourself and your responses accordingly (2 Corinthians 12:9).

5. Keep pressing on toward Jesus. Graveclothes are shed best as we pursue our friendship with Him. For as we fix our eyes on Jesus, we become less like us and more like Him (Psalm 34:5).

Forgetting what is behind and straining toward what is ahead, I press on toward the goal to win the prize for which God has called me heavenward in Christ Jesus.

PHILIPPIANS 3:13–14

10. Hebrews 12:12–13 speaks of strengthening the weak places in our lives and making "level paths" for our feet. What does Proverbs 4:23–27 have to say about this subject?

Practically speaking, what would making level paths look like in your life?

Make a Plan

James 5:16 tells us, "Therefore confess your sins to each other and pray for each other so that you may be healed." The early Methodists used to meet weekly for this type of accountability, asking each other probing questions. Take a few moments and work through these questions as honestly as possible:

Have you experienced any particular temptations during the past week?

How did you react or respond to those temptations?

Is there anything you are trying to keep secret, and if so, what?

Consider sharing your responses with a trusted friend and invite him or her to do the same. Then together take what you discover to the Lord in prayer.

Who I Am in Christ ...

Choose one of the statements from the "Who I Am in Christ" sidebar on pages 20–21 to meditate on. Write out the statement and the words of the accompanying verse. Work through the questions, then respond to God in prayer concerning the truth you've discovered.

Statement:

Verse:

What lie keeps you from accepting this as truth?

What does God's Word say about that?

Prayer:

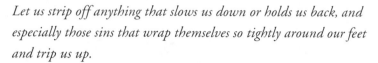

Session Seven Video

Shedding Graveclothes

> *Let us strip off anything that slows us down or holds us back, and especially those sins that wrap themselves so tightly around our feet and trip us up.*
>
> HEBREWS 12:1, TLB

Lazarus, Come Forth! John 11:17–44

When Jesus called Lazarus out of the tomb, the man was alive but still bound.

- Salvation—instantaneous
- Sanctification—a _____

Clothing Exchange, Ephesians 4:22–24

We have been made alive in Christ, but with the Spirit's help we must do our part.

- Put off our graveclothes by _____
- Put on His righteousness by _____

Beware the Snare, 2 Timothy 2:26

Whatever trips us can also entrap us. Snares[24] are:

1. Artfully _____

2. Usually attractive

3. Sadly _____

"Now to Him who is able to keep you from stumbling, and to present you faultless before the presence of His glory with exceeding joy" (Jude 1:24, NKJV).

Closing Time

I sense the Lord saying . . .

Prayer Requests

This Week's Assignment

- Follow through with your week 7 "Make a Plan" homework.
- Read chapters 9 and 10 in *Lazarus Awakening*.
- Answer week 8 study questions.
- Continue to review your verses. Memorize **1 John 5:11–12:** "And this is the testimony: God has given us eternal life, and this life is in his Son. He who has the Son has life; he who does not have the Son of God does not have life."

Living Resurrected

And if the Spirit of him who raised Jesus from the dead is living in you,
he who raised Christ from the dead will also give life to your mortal
bodies through his Spirit, who lives in you.

ROMANS 8:11

READ: Chapters 9 and 10 in *Lazarus Awakening*

*I*t's hard to believe that our time together is almost over. May I tell you how proud I am that you've finished this study? I know that life is busy, and it's hard to commit to an extended time like this. Especially when it involves being honest and open with God, and transparent with others as well as ourselves.

Yet nothing could be more important. When Jesus told His disciples He was going away to "prepare a place" for them in heaven, it was so that He could return to take them home to be with Him (John 14:2–3). Wouldn't it be wise, then, to invest our time here on earth preparing a place in our hearts and lives for Jesus so that He can be at home in us?

As we go forth from this study, it's my prayer that Jesus would be allowed to live within us in uninterrupted glory. That His life would be our life—and our life would be His. That we would leave our tombs behind and, with the Holy Spirit's help, purposefully shed our graveclothes. For it's time to wake up! It's time to live!

Memory Verse

And this is the testimony: God has given us eternal life, and this life is in his Son. He who has the Son has life; he who does not have the Son of God does not have life.

1 JOHN 5:11–12

ISRAEL MOMENT:
Jesus, the Resurrection and Life

When it comes down to it, everything hinges on whether or not Jesus's tomb was empty. As Paul wrote in 1 Corinthians 15:17, "If Christ has not been raised [from the dead], your faith is futile; you are still in your sins."

Amy Turnage and I discuss the many reasons we can be assured that the tomb was not only empty, but that Jesus rose from the dead!

REASONS TO BELIEVE IN THE RESURRECTION

1. Arguments for an empty tomb
   - Stolen body? Disciples were too afraid.
   - Wrong tomb? Authorities could have found the right one.
   - Robbery? Folded graveclothes make it unlikely.
2. Hundreds of witnesses (1 Corinthians 15:5–7)
3. Extrabiblical sources
   - Josephus in *Antiquities of the Jews* writes: "And many people from among the Jews and other nations became his disciples. Pilate condemned him to be crucified and to die. But those who had become his disciples did not abandon his discipleship. They reported that he had appeared to them three days after his crucifixion and that he was alive; accordingly, he was thought to be the Messiah concerning whom the prophets have recounted wonders. And the people of the Christians, named after him, have not disappeared till this day."[25]
4. Changed lives
   - Jesus's disciples and followers spent their lives spreading the gospel.
   - Many were martyred—people won't die for a lie.

Because of Adam and the Fall, we inherited death (Romans 5:17). But because of Jesus and His resurrection, the curse of death is broken. Our Savior conquered death, Revelation 1:18 tells us—and because Jesus lives, we live also!

THIS WEEK'S STUDY

1. Have you ever witnessed an amazing transformation brought about by Christ in someone else's life? Describe the changes and how they make you feel.

2. If you were asked to give a testimony of transformation in your life, what would you say? Perhaps you can't point to a finished work, but is there an attitude or behavior in which you're experiencing a measure of victory? (Don't discount baby steps. They are often God's method—the ordinary material He uses to work extraordinary miracles!)

3. Read John 15:1–8. Then, on pages 143–44 of *Lazarus Awakening,* read how Hudson Taylor's life and ministry was changed by his new understanding of these verses and the "exchanged life" Christ offers.

   With all that in mind, what is the difference between striving and abiding?

How would your life be different if you could learn to rest on the "Faithful One"?

4. When it comes to "dying to live," I listed some things that tend to be in direct opposition to Christ's rule and reign in my life. Which of the following do you struggle with? What other things would you add?

_____ A desire to control and direct my own life (and the lives of others)

_____ An expectation that I will be treated fairly at all times (and in all ways)

_____ A need to be well thought of by others (and thought of frequently)

_____ An insatiable appetite for escape (whether it be through food, television, books, or other avenues)

_____ Other:

_____ Other:

5. Read Galatians 2:20 slowly and prayerfully. Now read George Müller's "secret of service":

To one who asked him the secret of his service he said: "There was a day when I died, *utterly died*"; and, as he spoke, he bent lower and lower until he almost touched the floor—"died to George Müller, his opinions, preferences, tastes, and will—died to the world, its approval or censure—died to the approval or blame even of my brethren and friends—and since then I have studied only to show myself approved unto God."[26]

Using what you've discovered thus far in the study, write an obituary for yourself, renouncing the things that have held you back and declaring your decision to die so that Christ might live.

6. If you really believed that this world isn't all there is, how would it affect the way you view the following aspects of your life? (Write your response first, then consider the verses given.)

FINANCES:

Reflections on Matthew 6:19–21:

WORRIES:

Reflections on 2 Corinthians 4:17–18:

SICKNESS:

Reflections on 2 Corinthians 12:7–10:

HARDSHIPS:

Reflections on James 1:12:

PERSECUTION:

Reflections on Luke 6:22–23:

7. What do the following verses tell us about Jesus's return and the importance of being ready?

   Luke 12:35–40

   1 Thessalonians 5:1–6

   2 Peter 3:4, 8–14

8. Jesus promised that He would come back to take us to heaven so we could be together with Him (John 14:2–3). In light of that reality, consider the following questions:

   What do you imagine that day will be like?

   How close to Jesus do you hope to be?

Spiritually, what do you need to begin doing here on earth so that when that day comes, you can be known there as you are known here?

9. Please don't rush through this exercise. Take time to allow the truth of the following hymn, "The Love of God," to move from your head to your heart. Read the words slowly, then say or sing them again. Allow the immensity of the Father's love to wash over your heart. Accept it as truth. Rest in it. Revel in it. Receive it. Then write out a prayer asking the Holy Spirit to make God's love real in every corner of your soul.

The love of God is greater far
Than tongue or pen can ever tell;
It goes beyond the highest star,
And reaches to the lowest hell;
The guilty pair, bowed down with care,
God gave His Son to win;
His erring child He reconciled,
And pardoned from his sin.

Refrain:
O love of God, how rich and pure!
How measureless and strong!
It shall forevermore endure
The saints' and angels' song.

When years of time shall pass away,
And earthly thrones and kingdoms fall,
When men, who here refuse to pray,
On rocks and hills and mountains call,

God's love so sure, shall still endure,
All measureless and strong;
Redeeming grace to Adam's race—
The saints' and angels' song.

Could we with ink the ocean fill,
And were the skies of parchment made,
Were every stalk on earth a quill,
And every man a scribe by trade,
To write the love of God above,
Would drain the ocean dry.
Nor could the scroll contain the whole,
Though stretched from sky to sky.
    —Frederick M. Lehman[27]

My Response:

10. Looking back on your journey through this book study, what concept has made the biggest impact on you? In what ways has it changed the way you think or live?

Make a Plan

As we close this study, use the points listed in the sidebar on page 110 to create an action plan for "Living in the Light of Eternity."

Consider the following aspects of living resurrected, then list some practical ways you could begin to implement these mind-sets in your life right now.

LIVE FULLY:

HOLD THINGS LOOSELY:

VALUE PEOPLE HIGHLY:

TRAVEL LIGHTLY:

LOVE COMPLETELY:

GIVE FREELY:

LOOK EXPECTANTLY:

Which one do you want to focus on this week?

Write a short prayer asking God to help you keep an eternal point of view in the midst of your daily life.

Living in the Light of Eternity

In light of the fact that there is more to come, how then shall we live? If eternity, not this earth, is our true home, don't you think we should live differently than the world does? I'd like to suggest these principles:

- *Live fully.* Don't waste today regretting the past or fearing the future, for it may be your last day on earth. Make it count for God.
- *Hold things loosely.* Since we can't take our possessions with us, enjoy what you have, but don't cling so tightly to stuff or fall into the trap of always wanting more.
- *Value people highly.* People are the true treasures of life, worth nurturing and investing in, for they are the only thing on this earth we can possibly take with us when we leave.
- *Travel lightly.* Don't carry baggage from past hurts, and don't pick up grudges as you go. Life's too short to be voluntarily miserable.
- *Love completely.* Let God reveal His love for people through you. Be tender-hearted, not hardheaded, patient and quick to forgive, merciful and slow to judge.
- *Give freely.* Don't hoard what you have. Instead, share it with a joyful heart, and you'll be given more. Generosity releases blessings as sowing seed leads to harvest.
- *Look expectantly.* Keep looking up even as you walk here on earth, always ready and waiting for the imminent return of Christ. Be heavenly minded so you can be of earthly good.

*So then, dear friends, since you are looking
forward to [Christ's return], make every effort to
be found spotless, blameless and at peace with him.*

2 PETER 3:14

Who I Am in Christ ...

Choose one of the statements from the "Who I Am in Christ" sidebar on pages 20–21 to meditate on. Write out the statement and the words of the accompanying verse. Work through the questions, then respond to God in prayer concerning the truth you've discovered.

Statement:

Verse:

What lie keeps you from accepting this as truth?

What does God's Word say about that?

Prayer:

Session Eight Video

Light of Eternity

Fight the good fight of the faith. Take hold of the eternal life to which you were called.

1 TIMOTHY 6:12

Brought Back to Life, John 12:1–11

In this family from Bethany, I see a template for transformation:

- Lazarus _____.
- Martha _____.
- Mary _____.

A Threat to Hell, John 12:10–11 and Galatians 2:20

Don't you want your life to be a threat to hell like Lazarus's was? In order to live fully resurrected:

1. We must be willing to _____.

2. We must be willing to _____.

Eternity Starts Now! 1 Thessalonians 4:16–17

We don't have to wait for an end-time resurrection. Because of Jesus, we can live resurrected today.

"I have been crucified with Christ and I no longer live, but Christ lives in me. The life I live in the body, I live by faith in the Son of God, who loved me and gave himself for me" (Galatians 2:20).

Notes

Closing Time

I sense the Lord saying . . .

Personal Survey:

During the introduction week of the study, I asked you to give an honest evaluation of where you felt you were in your relationship with God. I'd like you to fill out the survey one more time, rating each statement with: O (Often); S (Sometimes); N (Never).

_____ I regularly sense/experience God's love for me.

_____ I feel distant from God.

_____ I feel secure in God's love.

_____ I think God loves me, but I don't feel it in my heart.

_____ I believe God loves other people, but I'm not entirely convinced He loves me.

_____ I'm learning to rely on God's love rather than my own worthiness.

_____ I feel God loves me less because of past failures and mistakes.

_____ I believe I am chosen and dearly loved by God.

Looking back at the initial survey, which, if any, of the statement ratings have changed?

What do you think caused the shift?

In what area(s) would you like to continue growing?

Prayer Requests

As We End This Study

It has been such a joy to be part of your life these past eight weeks. I hope you'll take what you've learned—both the spiritual truths and the practical tools—and continue to make yourself available to Jesus. Take time to sit at His feet. Allow Him to help you roll away any boulders of unworthiness, unforgiveness, or unbelief that might hinder your fellowship with Him. Continue to unwind your graveclothes and refuse to return to your tomb.

For "God, who is rich in mercy," Ephesians 2:4–5 tells us, has "made us alive with Christ." And the One who has awakened us will certainly teach us to live as we turn daily to Him.

I'd like to encourage you to do the following:

- Continue using the "Bible Reading Highlights" format (see page 123) to record what you hear God speaking to you from His Word. Use a journal or find additional pages at LazarusAwakening.com.
- Keep reviewing your memory verses, and consider adding more—for God's Word is "God-breathed," 2 Timothy 3:16–17 tells us, and it equips us "for every good work."
- Finish any study guide homework you were unable to complete.
- Go back through *Lazarus Awakening,* and mark things that impacted you. For easy access to meaningful material, consider writing the topic at the top of the page where it's found, or start an index inside the back cover with topics and page numbers.
- Invite a friend to go through the book with you again!

Whatever you do, please remember that you are precious to your heavenly Father. You were made for life, not death. So keep giving God access to your life. Keep taking baby steps. Because one day when we get to heaven, my friend, we are going to meet Jesus face to face. But that sweet kind of intimacy can begin today . . .

For eternity starts now!

The Story

John 11:1—12:11

John 11

¹Now a man named Lazarus was sick. He was from Bethany, the village of Mary and her sister Martha. ²This Mary, whose brother Lazarus now lay sick, was the same one who poured perfume on the Lord and wiped his feet with her hair. ³So the sisters sent word to Jesus, "Lord, the one you love is sick."

⁴When he heard this, Jesus said, "This sickness will not end in death. No, it is for God's glory so that God's Son may be glorified through it." ⁵Jesus loved Martha and her sister and Lazarus. ⁶Yet when he heard that Lazarus was sick, he stayed where he was two more days.

⁷Then he said to his disciples, "Let us go back to Judea."

⁸"But Rabbi," they said, "a short while ago the Jews tried to stone you, and yet you are going back there?"

⁹Jesus answered, "Are there not twelve hours of daylight? A man who walks by day will not stumble, for he sees by this world's light. ¹⁰It is when he walks by night that he stumbles, for he has no light."

¹¹After he had said this, he went on to tell them, "Our friend Lazarus has fallen asleep; but I am going there to wake him up."

¹²His disciples replied, "Lord, if he sleeps, he will get better." ¹³Jesus had been speaking of his death, but his disciples thought he meant natural sleep.

¹⁴So then he told them plainly, "Lazarus is dead, ¹⁵and for your sake I am glad I was not there, so that you may believe. But let us go to him."

¹⁶Then Thomas (called Didymus) said to the rest of the disciples, "Let us also go, that we may die with him."

¹⁷On his arrival, Jesus found that Lazarus had already been in the tomb for four days. ¹⁸Bethany was less than two miles from Jerusalem, ¹⁹and many Jews had come to Martha and Mary to comfort them in the loss of their brother. ²⁰When Martha heard that Jesus was coming, she went out to meet him, but Mary stayed at home.

²¹"Lord," Martha said to Jesus, "if you had been here, my brother would not have died. ²²But I know that even now God will give you whatever you ask."

²³Jesus said to her, "Your brother will rise again."

²⁴Martha answered, "I know he will rise again in the resurrection at the last day."

²⁵Jesus said to her, "I am the resurrection and the life. He who believes in me will live, even though he dies; ²⁶and whoever lives and believes in me will never die. Do you believe this?"

²⁷"Yes, Lord," she told him, "I believe that you are the Christ, the Son of God, who was to come into the world."

²⁸And after she had said this, she went back and called her sister Mary aside. "The Teacher is here," she said, "and is asking for you." ²⁹When Mary heard this, she got up quickly and went to him. ³⁰Now Jesus had not yet entered the village, but was still at the place where Martha had met him. ³¹When the Jews who had been with Mary in the house, comforting her, noticed how quickly she got up and went out, they followed her, supposing she was going to the tomb to mourn there.

³²When Mary reached the place where Jesus was and saw him, she fell at his feet and said, "Lord, if you had been here, my brother would not have died."

³³When Jesus saw her weeping, and the Jews who had come along with her also weeping, he was deeply moved in spirit and troubled. ³⁴"Where have you laid him?" he asked.

"Come and see, Lord," they replied.

³⁵Jesus wept.

³⁶Then the Jews said, "See how he loved him!"

³⁷But some of them said, "Could not he who opened the eyes of the blind man have kept this man from dying?"

[38]Jesus, once more deeply moved, came to the tomb. It was a cave with a stone laid across the entrance. [39]"Take away the stone," he said.

"But, Lord," said Martha, the sister of the dead man, "by this time there is a bad odor, for he has been there four days."

[40]Then Jesus said, "Did I not tell you that if you believed, you would see the glory of God?"

[41]So they took away the stone. Then Jesus looked up and said, "Father, I thank you that you have heard me. [42]I knew that you always hear me, but I said this for the benefit of the people standing here, that they may believe that you sent me."

[43]When he had said this, Jesus called in a loud voice, "Lazarus, come out!" [44]The dead man came out, his hands and feet wrapped with strips of linen, and a cloth around his face.

Jesus said to them, "Take off the grave clothes and let him go."

[45]Therefore many of the Jews who had come to visit Mary, and had seen what Jesus did, put their faith in him. [46]But some of them went to the Pharisees and told them what Jesus had done. [47]Then the chief priests and the Pharisees called a meeting of the Sanhedrin.

"What are we accomplishing?" they asked. "Here is this man performing many miraculous signs. [48]If we let him go on like this, everyone will believe in him, and then the Romans will come and take away both our place and our nation."

[49]Then one of them, named Caiaphas, who was high priest that year, spoke up, "You know nothing at all! [50]You do not realize that it is better for you that one man die for the people than that the whole nation perish."

[51]He did not say this on his own, but as high priest that year he prophesied that Jesus would die for the Jewish nation, [52]and not only for that nation but also for the scattered children of God, to bring them together and make them one. [53]So from that day on they plotted to take his life.

[54]Therefore Jesus no longer moved about publicly among the Jews. Instead he withdrew to a region near the desert, to a village called Ephraim, where he stayed with his disciples.

[55]When it was almost time for the Jewish Passover, many went up from the country to Jerusalem for their ceremonial cleansing before the

Passover. ⁵⁶They kept looking for Jesus, and as they stood in the temple area they asked one another, "What do you think? Isn't he coming to the Feast at all?" ⁵⁷But the chief priests and Pharisees had given orders that if anyone found out where Jesus was, he should report it so that they might arrest him.

John 12

¹Six days before the Passover, Jesus arrived at Bethany, where Lazarus lived, whom Jesus had raised from the dead. ²Here a dinner was given in Jesus' honor. Martha served, while Lazarus was among those reclining at the table with him. ³Then Mary took about a pint of pure nard, an expensive perfume; she poured it on Jesus' feet and wiped his feet with her hair. And the house was filled with the fragrance of the perfume.

⁴But one of his disciples, Judas Iscariot, who was later to betray him, objected, ⁵"Why wasn't this perfume sold and the money given to the poor? It was worth a year's wages." ⁶He did not say this because he cared about the poor but because he was a thief; as keeper of the money bag, he used to help himself to what was put into it.

⁷"Leave her alone," Jesus replied. "[It was intended] that she should save this perfume for the day of my burial. ⁸You will always have the poor among you, but you will not always have me."

⁹Meanwhile a large crowd of Jews found out that Jesus was there and came, not only because of him but also to see Lazarus, whom he had raised from the dead. ¹⁰So the chief priests made plans to kill Lazarus as well, ¹¹for on account of him many of the Jews were going over to Jesus and putting their faith in him.

Memory Verses

God's Word has the power to set us free, especially as we make it a part of our lives through memorization and application. Each week, you'll be assigned a memory verse to work on. If that is overwhelming, choose two or three verses to work on over the course of the study. A template of the verses is available online so you can download and print the verses for easy reference (LazarusAwakening.com).

Weeks One and Two

The thief does not come except to steal, and to kill, and to destroy. I have come that they may have life, and that they may have it more abundantly.

John 10:10, NKJV

Week Three

Yet to all who received him, to those who believed in his name, he gave the right to become children of God.

John 1:12

Week Four

"For I know the plans I have for you," declares the LORD, "plans to prosper you and not to harm you, plans to give you hope and a future."

Jeremiah 29:11

Week Five

Then Jesus said, "Did I not tell you that if you believed, you would see the glory of God?"

John 11:40

Week Six

But God demonstrates his own love for us in this: While we were still sinners, Christ died for us.

Romans 5:8

Week Seven

It is for freedom that Christ has set us free. Stand firm, then, and do not let yourselves be burdened again by a yoke of slavery.

Galatians 5:1

Week Eight

And this is the testimony: God has given us eternal life, and this life is in his Son. He who has the Son has life; he who does not have the Son of God does not have life.

1 John 5:11–12

Bible Reading Highlights

Where to Begin

If the concept of Bible Reading Highlights (described in "Word Time" in week 3 on page 26) is new to you, you may be wondering where to begin. All Scripture is inspired by God, but I've found some portions (Leviticus or Revelation, for instance) to be more overwhelming than others. When it comes to Bible meditation and personal application, here are some places you might start:

Proverbs—one chapter for each day of the month

Gospel of Mark—a great introduction to the life of Jesus

Galatians—a concise overview of the gospel message

Philippians—inspiration for victory in the midst of difficulty

James—practical advice for Christian living

1 John—an uplifting exploration of God's love

On the following pages you'll find Bible Reading Highlights templates to get you started.[28] Please feel free to photocopy these templates or go to LazarusAwakening .com to download additional pages in this format.

Date: _____ Portion I read today: _____

Best thing I marked today: Reference: _____

Verse: _____

_____

_____

How it impressed me: _____

_____

_____

_____

_____

Date: _____ Portion I read today: _____

Best thing I marked today: Reference: _____

Verse: _____

_____

_____

How it impressed me: _____

_____

_____

_____

_____

Date: _____ Portion I read today: _____

Best thing I marked today: Reference: _____

Verse: _____

_____

_____

How it impressed me: _____

_____

_____

_____

_____

Date: _____ Portion I read today: _____

Best thing I marked today: Reference: _____

Verse: _____

_____

_____

How it impressed me: _____

_____

_____

_____

_____

Date: _____ Portion I read today: _____

Best thing I marked today: Reference: _____

Verse: _____

_____

_____

How it impressed me: _____

_____

_____

_____

_____

Date: _____ Portion I read today: _____

Best thing I marked today: Reference: _____

Verse: _____

_____

_____

How it impressed me: _____

_____

_____

_____

_____

Date: _____ Portion I read today: _____

Best thing I marked today: Reference: _____

Verse: _____

_____

_____

How it impressed me: _____

_____

_____

_____

_____

Date: _____ Portion I read today: _____

Best thing I marked today: Reference: _____

Verse: _____

_____

_____

How it impressed me: _____

_____

_____

_____

_____

Date: _____ Portion I read today: _____

Best thing I marked today: Reference: _____

Verse: _____

_____

_____

How it impressed me: _____

_____

_____

_____

_____

Date: _____ Portion I read today: _____

Best thing I marked today: Reference: _____

Verse: _____

_____

_____

How it impressed me: _____

_____

_____

_____

Date: _____ Portion I read today: _____

Best thing I marked today: Reference: _____

Verse: _____

_____

_____

How it impressed me: _____

_____

_____

_____

_____

Date: _____ Portion I read today: _____

Best thing I marked today: Reference: _____

Verse: _____

_____

_____

How it impressed me: _____

_____

_____

_____

_____

Date: _____ Portion I read today: _____

Best thing I marked today: Reference: _____

Verse: _____

_____

_____

How it impressed me: _____

_____

_____

_____

_____

Date: _____ Portion I read today: _____

Best thing I marked today: Reference: _____

Verse: _____

_____

_____

How it impressed me: _____

_____

_____

_____

_____

Date: _____ Portion I read today: _____

Best thing I marked today: Reference: _____

Verse: _____

_____

_____

How it impressed me: _____

_____

_____

_____

_____

Date: _____ Portion I read today: _____

Best thing I marked today: Reference: _____

Verse: _____

_____

_____

How it impressed me: _____

_____

_____

_____

_____

Date: _____ Portion I read today: _____

Best thing I marked today: Reference: _____

Verse: _____

_____

_____

How it impressed me: _____

_____

_____

_____

_____

Date: _____ Portion I read today: _____

Best thing I marked today: Reference: _____

Verse: _____

_____

_____

How it impressed me: _____

_____

_____

_____

_____

Date: _____ Portion I read today: _____

Best thing I marked today: Reference: _____

Verse: _____

_____

How it impressed me: _____

_____

_____

_____

_____

Date: _____ Portion I read today: _____

Best thing I marked today: Reference: _____

Verse: _____

_____

_____

How it impressed me: _____

_____

_____

_____

_____

Date: _____ Portion I read today: _____

Best thing I marked today: Reference: _____

Verse: _____

_____

_____

How it impressed me: _____

_____

_____

_____

_____

Date: _____ Portion I read today: _____

Best thing I marked today: Reference: _____

Verse: _____

_____

_____

How it impressed me: _____

_____

_____

_____

_____

Notes

1. Adapted from *Growing Strong in God's Family: A Course in Personal Discipleship to Introduce New Life to Your Church,* the 2:7 Series (Colorado Springs: NavPress, 1987), 13, 19–20.

2. For more information on the Center for Holy Lands Studies and their programs to the lands of the Bible, go to www.holylandsstudies.org.

3. Referred to by Bargil Pixner, *With Jesus Through Galilee According to the Fifth Gospel* (Corazin, 1992), back cover.

4. Kim Trihey, conversation with author, date unknown.

5. Shlomo Pines, *An Arabic Version of the Testimonium Flavianum* (Jerusalem: Israel Academy of Arts and Sciences, 1971).

6. Nathan Bauman, "Aesop, Jesus, and Stories of Burying Money in the Ground," November 8, 2010, *West Coast Odysseus* (blog), http://nathan bauman.com/odysseus/?p=1523.

7. J. Levy, quoted in David Flusser, *The Sage from Galilee: Rediscovering Jesus' Genius,* 4th ed. (Grand Rapids, MI: Eerdmans, 2007), 14.

8. Adapted from Rosalind Goforth, *Climbing: Memories of a Missionary's Wife,* 2nd ed. (1940; repr., Elkhart, IN: Bethel, 1996), 80.

9. From Neil T. Anderson and Mike and Julia Quarles, *One Day at a Time: The Devotional for Overcomers* (Ventura, CA: Regal Books, 2000). Used by permission of Regal Books, a division of Gospel Light Publications. All rights reserved.

10. Francis Chan, *Crazy Love: Overwhelmed by a Relentless God* (Colorado Springs: David C. Cook, 2008), 110–11.

11. Charles H. Spurgeon, "A Mystery! Saints Sorrowing and Jesus Glad!" (sermon no. 585, Metropolitan Tabernacle, Newington, England, August 7, 1864), quoted in *Spurgeon's Sermons,* vol. 10, Christian Classics Ethereal Library, http://153.106.5.3/ccel/spurgeon/sermons10.xviii.html.

12. Pastor Don Burleson, "Big T-Truth" (sermon, New Covenant Fellowship, Kalispell, MT, June 8, 2008).

13. Warren Wiersbe, *The Wiersbe Bible Commentary: Old Testament,* 2nd ed. (Colorado Springs: David C. Cook, 2007), 755, emphasis in scriptures and outline format added.

14. "The Tel Dan Inscription: The First Historical Evidence of King David from the Bible," Bible History Daily, September 17, 2014, www.biblicalarchaeology .org/daily/biblical-artifacts/artifacts-and-the-bible/the-tel-dan-inscription -the-first-historical-evidence-of-the-king-david-bible-story/.

15. André Lemaire, "'House of David' Restored in Moabite Inscription," *Biblical Archaeology Review* 20, no. 3 (May/June 1994), www.cojs.org /pdf/house_of_david.pdf.

16. Marc Turnage, "The Pilate Inscription from Caesarea," March 25, 2013, *The Shard and the Scroll* (blog) http://theshardandthescroll.com/pilate -inscription/.

17. This is actually the subtitle of Groeschel's excellent book *The Christian Atheist: Believing in God but Living as If He Doesn't Exist* (Grand Rapids, MI: Zondervan, 2010).

18. Joyce Meyer, *Battlefield of the Mind: Winning the Battle in Your Mind* (1995; repr., New York: Warner Faith, 2002), 12.

19. Priscilla Shirer, *Discerning the Voice of God: How to Recognize When God Speaks* (Chicago: Moody, 2007), 14.

20. Oswald Chambers, *My Utmost for His Highest: The Golden Book of Oswald Chambers, Selections for the Year* (1935; repr., Westwood, NJ: Barbour, 1963), January 30, 20–21. Note: The bracketed phrase reflects an edit of the original text, which says, "God never speaks to us in startling ways." I made this adjustment in view of God's speaking to Moses through a burning bush, at Jesus's baptism, and other ways I consider startling.

21. Mrs. Charles [L. B.] Cowman, *Streams in the Desert,* February 9, www .christianity.com/devotionals/streams-in-the-desert/streams-in-the-desert -february-9th.html.

22. Special thanks to Marla Campbell, who shared this thought with me many years ago.

23. Josephus, *Jewish War* 2.446–51, http://theshardandthescroll.com/take upyourcross/.

24. Points adapted from a sermon given by C. H. Spurgeon, "The Bird Escaped from the Snare," number 1696, www.spurgeongems.org/vols28-30/chs1696 .pdf.

25. Pines, *Arabic Version of the Testimonium Flavianum,* 33.

26. Excerpt from a letter to J. Hudson Taylor, quoted in Arthur Tappan Pierson, *George Müller of Bristol* (1899; repr., Grand Rapids: Hendrickson, 2008), 383 (emphasis added).

27. Frederick Lehman, "The Love of God," 1917, public domain. Lehman "wrote this hymn in Pasadena, California, and it was published in *Songs That Are Different,* Volume 2, 1919. The lyrics are based on the Jewish poem *Haddamut,* written in Aramaic in 1050 by Meir Ben Isaac Nehorai, a cantor in Worms, Germany. The lyrics have been translated into at least eighteen languages," www.cyberhymnal.org/htm/l/o/loveofgo.htm.

28. Format adapted from *The Growing Disciple,* The 2:7 Series, Course 1 (Colorado Springs: NavPress, 1987), n.p.

Notes

Notes

Notes

Notes

Notes

Notes

Notes

Notes

Connect with Joanna

I'd love to hear from you at:
Facebook.com/BecomingHis
or by e-mail:
joannaweaver@hotmail.com

You can also write me at:
Joanna Weaver
PO Box 607
Hamilton, MT 59840

Other places to connect include:
JoannaWeaverBooks.com
LazarusAwakening.com

Draw Closer to Jesus

Go deeper into the familiar Bible stories of Mary, Martha, and Lazarus with Joanna's books *Having a Mary Heart in a Martha World*, *Having a Mary Spirit*, and *Lazarus Awakening*, each with companion study guides for personal or group use.

Video resources are also available via streaming or DVD.

You were made for more than serving God; you were made to know Him.

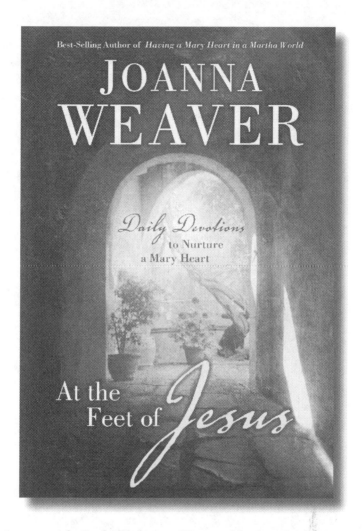

Intimacy with God—to know Him and be known by Him—is what our hearts desperately need, but somehow life conspires to keep us busy and distracted. *At the Feet of Jesus* offers 365 daily devotions to nurture your heart and move you toward a richer, more abundant life.

Printed in the United States
by Baker & Taylor Publisher Services